Dedication

To my grandchildren, Chloe, Jack, Lachlan, and Sophia. These beautiful children represent all young people because God loves each one and longs for their love in return.

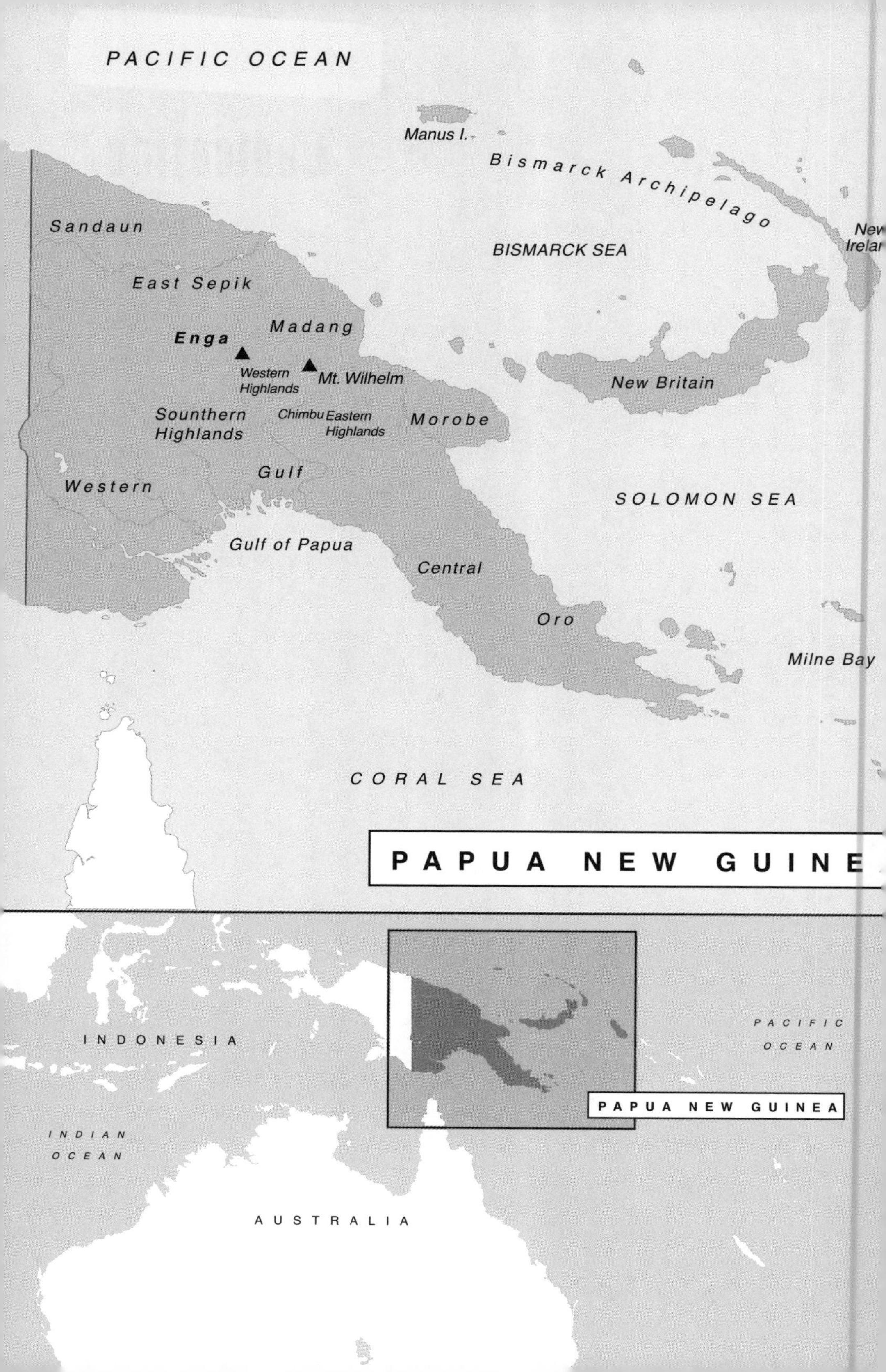

PACIFIC OCEAN

Manus I.

Bismarck Archipelago

BISMARCK SEA

New
Irelar

Sandaun

East Sepik

Madang

Enga ▲

Western
Highlands

Mt. Wilhelm ▲

New Britain

Sounthern
Highlands

Chimbu Eastern
Highlands

Morobe

SOLOMON SEA

Western

Gulf

Gulf of Papua

Central

Oro

Milne Bay

CORAL SEA

PAPUA NEW GUINE

INDONESIA

PACIFIC
OCEAN

PAPUA NEW GUINEA

INDIAN
OCEAN

AUSTRALIA

KEN VOGEL

The Fighter

 **Pacific Press®**
Publishing Association

Nampa, Idaho | Oshawa, Ontario, Canada
www.pacificpress.com

Cover design by Gerald Lee Monks
Cover design resources from the author
Inside design by Kristin Hansen-Mellish
Inside illustrations for chapters 1–10 are by Ken Dove

The author assumes full responsibility for the accuracy of all facts and quotations as cited in this book.

You can obtain additional copies of this book by calling toll-free 1-800-765-6955 or by visiting http://www.adventistbookcenter.com.

Library of Congress Cataloging-in-Publication Data:

Vogel, Ken, 1955-
  The fighter / Ken Vogel.
     pages cm
  ISBN 13: 978-0-8163-5715-4 (pbk.)
  ISBN 10: 0-8163-5715-3 (pbk.)
1. Piari, Paul. 2. Seventh-day Adventist converts—Papua New Guinea—Biography. 3. Seventh-day Adventists—Missions—Papua New Guinea. I. Title.
  BX6189.P53V64 2015
  286.7092—dc23
  [B]
                              2014042842

March 2015

Acknowledgments

Pastor Paul Piari told the following story to Pastor Ken Vogel when they worked together in the 1980s. His story was recorded on tape, then later transcribed and translated by the author to become the core facts for this book.

Pastor Paul's family members have provided invaluable detail essential to the story's continuity. In particular, appreciation is given to Paul Piari's wife, Dorcas, and daughter Jane (Wason). Where there is a difference of memory between Paul and that of the family, this book is true to Paul's own account.

In order to relate the Engan culture as accurately as possible, the author has also secured the advice of Joseph Talipuan. Joseph himself is an Engan from the Wabag region and has worked as a Seventh-day Adventist pastor in many areas of the Enga, including the Lagaip Valley. He has given special study to the traditional beliefs of the various Engan tribes. Joseph has verified the spelling and translation of Engan expressions and has provided many Engan cultural and traditional religious details.

Historical data not included in Pastor Piari's interviews was gleaned from *A Family Album of the Enga Adventist Jubilee 1944–1994,* compiled by Samuel Joseph Kopamu and edited by Laurence A. Gilmore.

The illustrations capturing key elements of the story within chapters 1 through 10 are the work of Ken Dove.

Appreciation is extended to Marlene Vogel for the simple illustrations that make it easier to visualize some things described in the Fact Files.

Special thanks to the Adventist Heritage Centre, Cooranbong, NSW, Australia, for their assistance with the artifacts used in the cover illustration.

And a very special thanks to Ashrie Talipuan for his willingness to model the traditional dress from his tribe.

Contents

Preface

As was the case with Piari, the culture in which young people grow up can often conflict with God and His ways. But God is patient and will not give up on anyone. He is close by, even when you think He might not be. His love drives His longing for you to make your own choice to follow Him.

Pastor Ken Vogel

Introduction

Whether in ancient times or modern, the role of the warrior or soldier who goes into battle is glorified. But when it comes to recognizing bravery, interestingly, often the highest awards and accolades go to those who have risked their own lives in order to save others, rather than kill.

This story is about one particular warrior. He starts out enjoying the adrenaline and excitement of the fight and the kill. But when I knew Piari, he had become a warrior of a different kind. He did not live for killing, excitement, and self-glory. Instead of being intent on killing others, he changed and risked his own life to save others!

What was it that changed this fierce warrior?

He came to know Jesus as his personal Savior and best Friend! He became a warrior in a totally different sense—God's warrior, a missionary for God.

And this makes Piari the bravest of warriors, because, rather than go to the front of the battle to kill, he eventually went to the front of the battle to save and to serve. May every young reader also make that choice.

While this book is Piari's story, it is also about Adventist mission. God prepared the way for Piari through the influence of his father and mother and the oral transmission of truth. God was then able to influence this young man's life through Christian missionaries and truth as found in the Holy Bible.

Pastor Ken Vogel

Fact File

Piari, the central character of this true story, is from the Lagaip Valley, which is within the Enga Province of Papua New Guinea.

The setting is the highlands of Papua New Guinea, from the 1940s through the late 1950s.

Great change was taking place in Papua New Guinea through this period, with much of the interior being opened up to the wider world for the first time.

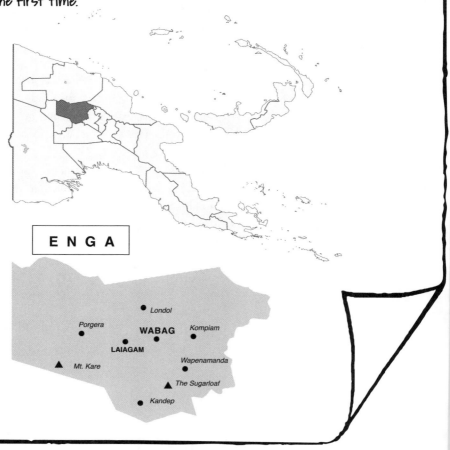

Chapter One

Piari flattened himself on the sun-dappled jungle floor, his chest heaving. *Did they hear me? Will they see me?* His bow and a fistful of arrows lay uncomfortably under him where he had quickly dropped.

The enemy tribe would not hesitate to kill him were they to find him. What he did was crazy! Even a much older and more experienced warrior would rarely do what Piari had just done. Tribal warfare in the Enga was unpredictable. But normally the warriors stay linked to their fight leader. While serious injury and death was inflicted on the enemy in this way, it was the unexpected that could deal the exceptional blow. And that was what Piari wanted. And that was what he was about to achieve. But the late arrival of some enemy warriors on the path blocked his move to get behind his target and attack from behind.

Much later, Piari appeared back at Niungu, his home village. Some of his friends saw him approach the village and met him with a chorus of voices. "Piari! Piari! You made it! Hey, you're OK!"

Hearing the commotion, his mother, Titam, ran out. "Where have you been? We all thought you had been injured or even killed!"

Pulling him by his ear, Titam dragged Piari toward their hut, a typical, low-sitting grass-roofed hut. This would-be man quickly remembered he was still a boy. He knew resistance would be to no avail. The subdued golden glow from the internal fire of this windowless wood, bark, and grass structure added intensity as this desperate mother challenged her twelve-year-old son. "The other warriors returned not knowing where you were. We all thought you had been speared—or worse!"

"Oh, Mother, I fight for the protection and honor of our tribe," Piari responded. Completely ignoring his mother's concern, he continued with great relish. "And I nearly got behind the enemy this time. If those enemy warriors hadn't come along, I could have killed more of our enemy today!"

A shadow fell over the low, small entrance to the hut. Piari's father, Nun (the

The Fighter

"u" pronounced as in *full*), crouched and nimbly moved inside. He sat down cross-legged by the fire. Piari didn't look up. He knew exactly what look his father was giving him.

"Piari! Fighter!" his father growled. "We named you Amusa, which means 'the bush holds together forever,' so that you will be the father of a strong and united family that continues on into the future. But the village people have tagged you with this new name because you are getting much fame as a warrior. Piari—the fighter! Piari—warrior! I fear this name will stay with you all your life. But it may be a short life."

Nun reached out his muscular arm and deftly grabbed hold of Piari's hair before the boy knew it. *"Idi hup!"* Nun said with deep emotion. "God hold on to you from now on! The God who lives in the land of mystery will place a heavy burden on your head." This old, wise, and God-fearing father knew that God would not give up on the boy, no matter how long it took to draw him to Himself.

Tribal fighting was a part of life in the Lagaip Valley of what is now the Enga Province of Papua New Guinea. It was thought that if there was no payback for something done by neighboring tribes, such perceived weakness would mean more trouble, possibly threatening the very existence of the tribe.

And so the men would plan their attack in the days leading up to the fight. During the nights, the valleys would echo with the strong Engan calls from mountaintops, declaring the fight. Well before the sun warmed the mountain air—frigid even in the tropics at seventy-two hundred feet above sea level—warriors would light small fires, rub pig fat over their bodies, and chant and stomp their feet rhythmically while armed with spears and shields or bows and arrows. As the sun came up, these warriors, having psyched themselves into a frenzy, would move out to the fighting front.

Piari was a member of the Piolai clan of the Piapri tribe. This was one of the few Engan tribes that allowed uninitiated boys to participate in the fighting. Not many boys got involved, but Piari was at the head of the pack. He already had a number of kills to his name. Piari, the fighter!

But while Piari was at the center of any fighting, his father, Nun, was not. Opposed to fighting, he constantly urged his tribe to resolve conflict in other ways. Nun worshiped God as his father and grandfather had. The ancestors of the Engan people always believed in a great, good eternal God who lives in the land of mystery.

Yet most of the tribe had allowed superstition and fear to have the last word, which gave the evil one control over their lives. Piari's father was different. He really believed in God. And he believed that life was sacred. Nun regularly worshiped God and made sacrifices to Him.

The other boys in the village listened with wide eyes as Piari recounted his escapades, more interested in joining his audience than in joining the fighting. Engans are master storytellers, and Piari was no exception. Emerging from the family hut, he would see the boys gathered at the guava tree and race over to them. His father's pleas disappeared behind his friends' eager faces as Piari strutted up to his friends.

"You should have seen us! The Niungu warriors were faster than our enemy—those weaklings. Our spears and arrows were on target. We had it all over them. We moved as one from among the tall casuarina trees. The enemy warriors were like scared grasshoppers, hopping about but going nowhere. Haru, your father raced forward and shot an arrow straight at the enemy fight leader. He got him—I'm *sure* he did. Did you hear their cry go up? We got one of them, all right!"

Piari's face beamed as he relived the excitement of the fight. "When I saw their momentary confusion and the focus on their fight leader, I got an idea. I raced along the side of the gully and across to the other side. The jungle was dense, but I pushed through to get in behind the enemy."

"That's crazy, Piari," his best friend, Nala, interrupted. "We have been taught to stay together in the fight. You shouldn't do that."

"Not normally, Nala. But what an opportunity when they were confused and distracted!"

Nala's mother called him to bring firewood. It was getting late, and the thick white smoke of the fires pressed through the grass roofs of each *hauskuk* (small cooking hut) as the women prepared food in the soot-blackened, earthenware pots. The group of boys slowly dissipated as they walked back to their huts. In a way, Piari was glad that he did not have to tell the rest of his story. This way he could save face. He knew the boys envied his spirit, and he loved fighting. He was truly Piari—fighter. Piari—warrior!

Fact File

Papua New Guinea is a nation comprising the eastern half of the island of New Guinea, just north of Australia.

With a population of around 7.5 million, well over eight hundred languages are spoken in this small country, about 12 percent of all the world's languages.

The Enga Province is home to one of the larger language and cultural groups in Papua New Guinea.

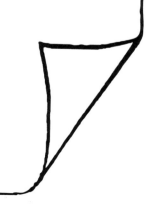

Chapter Two

Catch me if you can!" Nala shouted back to Piari. This short but muscular Engan boy moved like lightning through the dense jungle, jumping sprightly across a gully just when it seemed the game was up.

Piari was not to be outdone. "I can, Nala! You'll see. I will catch you, no matter how long it takes," he rejoined, laughing loudly. Like Nala, Piari was very fit, as were all highland boys of Papua New Guinea. But even the fit have their limits.

Nala was struggling to keep going but was also reticent to let Piari win. Puffing as he yelled back, Nala shouted, "When will you give up, Piari?"

"Ha! Never, Nala. Never! You know that," yelled Piari. It was true, and Nala did know it. Piari was not one to give up on anything!

Soon after, Nala dropped to the ground in exhaustion. Piari quickly arrived and toppled over beside him. Both boys were puffing profusely but also laughing. They were great friends and still enjoyed the opportunity for a game. But as they grew older, there was less and less time for games, with adultlike chores being expected of them.

They lay on their backs, enjoying the majesty of the motley green jungle canopy above them while they caught their breath.

"Wow! Look at that!" Piari whispered loudly, pointing with his chin high up in a tall jungle softwood tree with large branches spreading out nearly horizontally from the main trunk.

"Yes! I can see it," Nala nodded. "The man bird of paradise is trying to get the attention of the girl bird. Ha ha! Will she like his dance today?"

The boys lay there, transfixed by the male ribbon-tailed bird of paradise, a shiny black bird with two huge, pure white, ribbonlike tail feathers. The drabber female flitted about on the branches nearby while the male began his courtship dance. He strutted back and forth along a large branch. Then he began flicking and swirling his long tail feathers in an impressive artistic display. They had seen these magnificent birds many times but had never stopped to watch the courtship dance. It went on for several minutes.

"What girl bird would not respond to that?" Nala exclaimed. A moment later, Piari pointed and said, "That one." They couldn't believe their eyes as the female bird of paradise flew off, clearly unimpressed.

"You just can't please girls, can you, Nala?" Piari groaned. The boys laughed as they watched the male begin his pursuit, having difficulty gaining much altitude due to his heavy tail feathers. The boys got up and wandered in the direction of the village.

"My father told me the story of how the birds and the trees came in the beginning. God must have had fun making all these things," Nala said thoughtfully as he reflected on what had just transpired.

"Mmm," mumbled Piari.

"You don't sound convinced. What's going on in that head of yours, my friend?" Nala tilted his head as he looked at Piari and waited for his answer.

Piari replied slowly, "Oh, I don't know. My father tells me about the law of that same God. And if I believe the stories of beginnings, then maybe I should obey the law. Oh, forget it. Let's see who can get back to the village first!"

With that, Piari was off, with Nala right behind him, laughing. "I'll beat you this time, Piari!"

Back at the village, the boys were quickly called upon to restock the firewood in the *haus man* (where the men and boys slept).

Piari's conversation with Nala returned to his mind. His father did not want him to fight and kill. And he said that this was because it was in the law of God that people should not kill each other. *Father is no wimp,* Piari thought to himself. *He is a strong and brave man. So if he does not go into battle like the others, there has to be another reason. Mmmm. Father respects his God that much!*

These thoughts were not heading in the direction that young, impulsive, and adrenaline-driven Piari liked. So he quickly replaced them with thoughts about the thrill of the fight, weapons, and strategic action. He loved the fight. He lived for it.

That was his life—Piari, fighter!

Fact File

Ribbon-tailed bird of paradise (Astrapia mayeri)

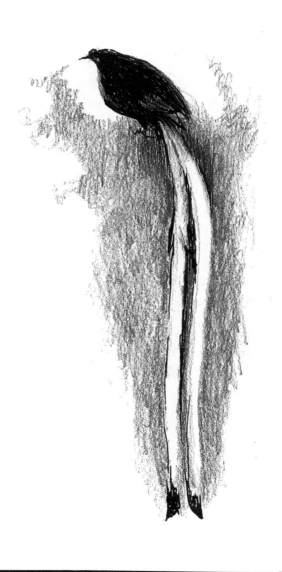

Chapter Three

Flames licked the last piece of firewood in the *hauskuk*. Their orange hue joined with the bright-red embers lying under it all to cast familiar shadows against the soot-black roof. Nun's family had eaten well, *kaukau* and cooking banana having been baked in the fire itself and the silver fern having been cooked in the earthenware pot.

"We have a special work to start tomorrow as a family," Nun declared. This got the children's attention. Normally, family activities segregated the men and the women. "Together?" asked Kainkali, the eldest child. The four children were all ears.

Nun continued without addressing Kainkali's query. "Amusa! Or maybe you respond more to 'Piari' these days." Piari felt uncomfortable as everyone looked at him. His father continued, "You might think fighting helps protect our tribe. But there is much more to our future than you realize."

Titam took over at this point, using a typical Engan *tokbokis* (story) to make a point. "You eat lots of *kaukau* because it is the best food that grows high up in the mountains where we live. But have you eaten only *kaukau* tonight? No. You have had other food as well—banana and fern. Your father has always emphasized the importance of different food from the garden and bush. This variety gives us strength and health."

Where is this heading? thought Piari, his head spinning as he tried to understand the point of his mother's *tokbokis*.

Nun took over. "While many of us see tribal warfare as protection from abuse by neighboring tribes, it by no means guarantees our future."

Piari squirmed as his older brother delighted in his discomfort. "Yes," Kainkali said. "You listen carefully to Mother and Father, Piari."

But Nun immediately put Kainkali in his place. "And you are out there fighting at every opportunity, too, my firstborn son! You also need to listen carefully." Kainkali's smile quickly dissolved.

"Indeed, a man gains respect and status in our tribe by his skill as a warrior.

The Fighter

But there is much more to it than that: oratory skill, business skill, and even the number of wives (which I don't agree with myself)." The children knew they dare not interrupt their father. He was on a roll.

"Your mother and I have tried to teach you the important things in life: gardening, toolmaking, hunting, building, medicine, helping others," Nun said earnestly.

Titam interjected, "Tomorrow we begin to teach you something that is very different. If you learn this, you and your families will be able to trade with tribes beyond our valley. Tomorrow we are going to begin the long task of making bush salt." Bush salt was a rare treat; the children knew this was a thing of great value.

Nun continued, "The source of this bush salt is rare. But on our family land there is a water spring from which it is made. There is much demand, even by faraway tribes."

Piari's sister, Sanison, leaned forward eagerly. "What do they give us if we give them some of our bush salt?"

Nun's serious face now broadened into a wide grin. "It may be that we will be able to trade a cake of our bush salt for a *kina* shell." Even Piari was on board now, immediately lost in pleasant thoughts of wearing a *kina* shell to a *singsing*.

Nun continued, "To start with, the boys and I have to go high into the mountains to our family land, as there is some heavy preparation before we all go there as a family to make the salt. Piapin, you are coming too," Nun said to Piari's younger brother with a chuckle in his voice.

Piapin hadn't shown much interest in the travel plans because he expected to have to stay home with his mother and sister, as usual. But then he heard his name! While it was hard for Piari and Kainkali to sleep that night, Piapin especially struggled to settle down. Adrenaline kept the three of them awake with the anticipation of exploring new land and learning new skills, but this would be Piapin's very first serious activity with his father! Finally, each of the boys' thoughts died out along with the embers in the fireplace.

The next morning found three boys excitedly discussing the possibility of owning a kina shell. Only a few families in the clan had one of these precious items. No one knew its origin. It was traded by distant tribes, who said they received it in trade from even more distant tribes. There was some notion of it coming from an immense body of water. But all this was beyond their capacity to comprehend, and beyond the comprehension of anyone in the tribe. No one had ever traveled beyond their region.

Nun interrupted their chatter. "We must plan now for our long journey ahead, boys. Each of you be sure your stone axe is sharp and strapped strongly into its handle."

Piapin looked down. His excitement to be going with the others was all but snuffed out as he thought, *I don't have a stone axe.*

"Why such a long face, Piapin?" A glint of joyful mischief played in his father's voice.

Still looking down, the downcast boy hadn't noticed his father's inflection, as everyone else had. Titam smiled happily, knowing what was about to happen.

There, raised high in Father's hand was a brand-new stone axe! "The old men made this while we have been felling trees. They have selected a strong stone and have chipped and rubbed away at its edge till it is sharp. And they have wedged it into the wooden handle and strapped it tightly so it won't come out. It is for you, Piapin."

"Oh, Father! *Yakapalinooooooooo!* Thank you, thank you, thank you!" Piapin's grin could not have filled his mouth with a bigger smile. Not only did this mean his very own stone axe, but it also signified that his father and the elders saw him as old enough to begin doing some things with the men.

"But save using it until we get up into the mountains, Piapin. In the meantime, you help your mother with preparations for our journey," Nun instructed. "Kainkali and Piari, you and I have much work to do to cut extra firewood for Mother and Sanison while we are away. We will be away from the village for many days." The boys looked at each other. This sounded like an even bigger adventure than they first thought.

Three days later, in the cold of the early morning of the highlands, as the smoke filtered through the roofs of the many huts scattered behind their village security fencing, Nun gathered his team of boys. Piapin had the fire stick, a *billum* full of food, and his new prized stone axe, of course! Piari had his weapons, his stone axe, and his *billum* filled with food, as did Kainkali and Nun.

Two elders, shivering in the freezing morning air, walked into the small compound. They brought a gift for this important journey. It was important for the immediate family, as well as for the village and the clan. They each held out two stones, carefully crafted for stone axes. What a gift! But that is what life in a traditional Engan village was all about. Everyone looked out for each other. What was important to one was important to the others.

The gift of these stones could save days of work for Nun and his boys. Without them, if a stone broke—and they often would—they would have to stop their work, find a new stone, and carefully craft it into a cutting edge for the axe.

With encouragement from all, the four set out. Nun smiled because he was helping his boys to learn and grow. Piari and his brothers smiled because they were embarking on the greatest adventure of their lives.

Fact File

Kina and toea are the names given to modern-day Papua New Guinean currency. There are one hundred toea in one kina. Kina and toea are actually saltwater shellfish. Originally, these shells were traded from tribe to tribe, starting with the coastal tribes. As each tribe traded these shells with their more inland neighbors, the value grew. All tribes-but especially the tribes of the isolated interior highlands-placed great value on these shells, especially on the beautiful kina shell.

Kina

Toea

Engans traditionally had a stone axe for killing and a stone axe for felling and splitting timber.

Working axe

Chapter Four

The start of the journey covered familiar terrain. But it was not long before Nun turned up a less worn path toward the southern mountain peaks.

Excitement grew among the brothers. Piapin would run ahead, anticipating the direction his father would take. Kainkali faithfully kept a few paces behind his father. Piari kept up the rear, ever watchful in case of danger.

Their short but very muscular father kept up a fast and constant pace. He knew that there was a lot of distance to cover. After a couple of hours, each of the three boys threw aside any daydreams and unnecessary forays. The going was tough, the terrain becoming far more steep and rugged. The slippery clay from the wet season rains made it even more difficult, and even these fit boys began to tire. But their pride and excitement meant no one was going to complain or dawdle. As the day wore on, they covered a tremendous distance before Nun brought his boys to a halt.

In front of them was a deep gully, through which fast and furious water boiled in its rush down the mountain. This water was being fed from higher up in the mountains, and, being wet season, was at its peak of fill and energy.

"Do not try to traverse this gully on that vine bridge, boys!" Nun directed. All three boys had already decided on caution. Piari and Kainkali recalled the death of one of the village boys who fell into such a raging gully. He had been swept away with no hope of getting out. The sight of his battered and bruised body at his funeral left a deep and lasting impression.

Father's voice interrupted their thoughts. "We built this bridge the last time we came up here, which was a very long time ago. It will need some careful repairs so that it is strong and safe for when we return with your mother and sister."

A couple of hours later this party of four was safely across the gully and heading farther into territory new to the boys. As they walked, Nun pointed out plants and trees that grew only in this area, explaining what was safe to eat and what could be made from them. When the whole family would arrive here in several months, they would spend more time on such matters. But for now, the focus was on getting to the site, setting up a bush camp, and felling trees.

As the dark and cold of night began to fall, Nun and his three sons collected firewood for a little warmth. They would sleep around a small fire that would ease the freezing cold for at least one side of their bodies.

There was no need for Nun to stir his boys to rise the next morning, because the fire had gone out and they were wide awake from the bitter cold. "No. Don't relight the fire, Kainkali. We must get going," Nun said as he gathered his *billum,* axe, and bow and arrows.

Well before first light, they hiked through dense jungle. Only the extraordinary capacity of the highlander to see even in the darkest night made this possible. Later, with the sun high above them, Nun and his boys reached the special area for making bush salt. Excitement grew again among all three boys as they noticed that this site, while overgrown, had obviously been a scene of activity on many occasions in the past. It was impossible for them to get their minds around their own father's reflections that his father had made bush salt here, as had his father's father and his father's father's father before that.

The first task was to make bush shelters. They needed to be sturdy, because they would use them again in a few months when the whole family would return to complete the task. But before the rest of the day was taken up with such construction, Nun led the boys in the direction of the stand of softwood trees that were needed for making the bush salt.

"Father, these trees look the same as the ones down near our village," Piari questioned, his eyebrows furrowed.

Nun's broad face and large lips smiled. "Yes, Amusa. It is not the tree that makes the difference, but the water." He led his boys farther on toward a very damp area with channels cut into it. Nothing but a tough and nearly colorless moss grew there. Pointing to this damp area, Nun declared triumphantly, "This is what makes the difference."

Each of the boys turned toward where Nun was pointing, looked at each other quizzically, and looked again at the damp, moss-covered area. Piari spoke first. "Where is the bush salt? Do we cook the moss?"

Nun gave a hearty laugh. Not to lose the opportunity to give his brother a hard time, Kainkali also laughed loudly. "So what do you think, Kainkali?" Nun quickly asked, so as to avoid an otherwise inevitable clash between the brothers. Kainkali quickly stopped his laughter, because he had no idea.

"It is in the water, boys!" said Nun. "It is in the water." Then he bent down and pressed his thick hands through the moss into the damp soil beneath. Pushing the soil aside, he made a small depression. Very quickly this depression began filling with water. The boys took turns tasting it. Reactions varied from frowns to spitting it out.

Here was Nun's opportunity. "I am glad my ancestors did not do what you have just done and turn away in disgust. This mineral salt not only helps food taste great, but it is also a strong medicine. And God from the land of mystery is like this water. He brings meaning to our lives and is medicine for our people. But too many, Amusa, turn their back on Him because they don't like how He tastes at first."

Piari understood the lesson his father was directing especially at him. Wanting to move on, he asked, "So how do we make bush salt from that mineral water?" Nun was not finished with his lesson, and his son had unknowingly stepped right in the direction Nun was heading.

He responded, "The water has to be absorbed into the timber, just like God must be absorbed into your life. Normally, softwood is not much good because it cannot withstand insects and weather. But when it is filled with this mineral water, it is of great value. Your life is of great value when you let God be part of it."

It was now time for action. Nun began explaining the whole process for making cakes of bush salt. The boys listened carefully as their father explained, "We will cut down some trees and split the timber. Then we will bring the timber up here and lay them in channels we make in the damp area. That is our task here this time. We will leave them for a couple of cycles of the moon so they can absorb this mineral water."

He continued, "I will then send you, Kainkali and Amusa, back here on your own to take the timber out of the damp and stand them to dry. Once they have had time to dry, then we will all return as a family, including your mother and sister. Only then can we make cakes of bush salt. I will explain the final step later."

The next day, the really hard work began. Nun took young Piapin as his tree-felling partner, while Kainkali joined with Piari. It became a competition, with Piari, ever the competitive one, pushing his older brother harder and harder.

At long last, after two days, Nun and his youngest son had felled their first tree and split it. They had just begun chopping into their second when all of a sudden Nun yelled, "There's a possum in this tree, boys!"

As he said this, a large possum leaped from the hollow where it had its home. There was a scramble as all four—even Nun—raced to catch this prize. Possum fur is a valued addition to the bush string that is used in making warm Engan knitted hats and men's *billums*.

Laughter echoed down the valley as the chase continued. Then a whoop of delight erupted from Kainkali, the victor.

Chapter Five

Several months passed. Kainkali and Piari had returned to the mineral salt site and had laid the now-saturated timber out to dry, preparing it to burn. It was time for the family to go and finally make the sought-after bush salt.

Morning light begrudgingly made its entrance through mist that hung like a heavy wet blanket over the trees. Smoke filtering through the grass roofs of the many huts could not go upward, so it spread itself sideways. This haze draped the normally vivid green of the surrounding jungle in soft pastel colors. The world seemed to move in slow motion. But there was at least one family that could not be charmed into this mode.

As the Nun family stirred and prepared for their journey, the whole village began merging toward their compound. They were all aware and excited, as well. It was not every day that bush-salt making made the agenda. Eventually, both the *haus man* and the *haus meri* were wrapped in a buzz of noise, with children running and laughing and adults talking excitedly.

"Piari. Leave those fighting arrows behind," called Nun.

Why is it that fathers seem to have eyes all around their heads? Piari thought.

His father continued, "But be sure to bring two bird arrows with you."

"Piapin, you bring the fire stick. Your mother will prepare it for you. Each of us will carry food that your mother has prepared for our journey." Titam and Sanison had baked some *kaukau* and wrapped them, still hot, in banana leaves tied up with vine.

The girls were ready by the time the boys joined them. Excitement grew as they saw their mother and sister standing there, each with a heavy *billum* on her back, with the weight taken by the strap over their head and placed against the forehead. They automatically hunched forward to keep balance. Piapin was given some food to put in his *billum*.

As the villagers filtered back to their own regular activity, Nun and his family made their way along the mountain track. Some small children ran beside them for a while, giggling and laughing. But soon they tired and made their way back to their mothers. Nun and his family steadily moved on, initially following the well-trodden track. The heavy mist did not faze Nun. He knew the path well. The morning calls of the birds seemed to have a hollow sound to them in this thick air. Bare feet that were used to such tracks easily coped with stones and sticks on the path, which was narrow at times. This family was very fit and nimbly traversed the path, even where it was steep with a thousand-foot drop on one side.

"It is getting brighter, Father." Piapin sounded glad to experience the lifting of the mist's darkness.

"Yes," returned Nun. "We have climbed a long way up the mountain. So we might soon see blue sky." And just as he said that, there was a momentary glimpse of blue as the breeze blew the mist aside, only to return it just as quickly.

"It is cold up here," Sanison whimpered as she rubbed her hands together.

"Yes," Nun agreed. "We are nearing the altitude where the *karuka* nut grows. *Mmmm.* Wouldn't it be great if it were the time to harvest this nut? We could have made a campfire and roasted them. They are scrumptious."

"Oh, Father!" exclaimed Kainkali. "Stop it! You are making me hungry! Oh, how I love the *karuka* nut!"

Titam chuckled at this family banter. She loved her family and was glad for this special occasion to pass life skills on to the children.

Piari was thinking in another direction. *The* karuka *nut is not only tasty, it is also of great value to us. If anyone from another tribe came into our area and harvested our* karuka, *we would go into battle.* He could not keep quiet, so he proclaimed, "I will protect our *karuka.* If anyone tried to take them, I would kill them!"

At this Titam's peaceful joy was harshly replaced by tense fear. What could she do to help her dear son change his life focus?

Her troubled mind was quickly interrupted by the stern voice of Nun. "Amusa—the bush holds together forever. Piari—warrior. Who are you, my son? The family and tribe hold together in more ways and often better ways than fighting! But it seems that Piari will always be part of your name. Only the great God who lives in the land of mystery can help you!"

Silence descended on this family of six as they steadily continued. Fortunately, it was not too much longer until they broke out of the mist just prior to reaching the top of the ragged ridge. This seemed to lift everyone's spirits again.

It was time to stop and enjoy the *kaukau* Titam had cooked very early in the morning. The food was now cold, but that was how they often ate it when working or walking. No one minded. The flavor, sweetness, and nourishment of this staple food was enjoyed by all.

Somewhere a long way below, their fellow villagers were already well established into their daily routine. But Nun and his family had a special task ahead of them, and they had to cover a lot more ground over two days before they could begin.

The makeshift bush shelters that Nun and his sons had constructed many months earlier were a welcome sight to the tired family when they arrived late in the evening. The next morning, the whole family was busy with allocated tasks as they constructed a temporary camp for the few days they would be there to make the bush salt.

The first thing, though, was to make a fire. It was even colder than in Niungu in this high-altitude valley more than ten thousand feet above sea level. Each person held their arms across their chests to keep in some body warmth.

"Come on. Make the fire big so I can be warm," Piapin urged Kainkali.

"Well, do what Father told you and collect some firewood," retorted Kainkali. The fire was easier to get going because there were still hot coals from overnight. But starting the fire the previous evening had not been so easy because they had to use the fire stick Piapin had brought, and it was hard to find dry wood at night.

Nun spoke. "We will all collect firewood together."

Piapin showed some reluctance because he was still tired from the long walk. "Yes, Piapin, you come too," said Father.

Piari jostled his little brother and gave him a push. But that look from his father made it clear he should back off. Reluctantly, Piapin joined the others as they made their way into the jungle in search of firewood.

They heard some familiar sounds around them on the mountainside of this valley as they searched. But there were some unfamiliar ones, as well. As a bird that was new to the children flew into view, questions flew right alongside it. The previous evening, they had seen a different kind of possum, and Father had explained what he knew about it. This is how learning took place at this time. Father and Mother would pass on what had been passed on to them by their parents and what they had themselves learned in life.

Once the firewood was collected along with some jungle food, Nun and Titam sat down with their children and described the final process for making the bush salt. Nun concluded, "Other tribes do not have this knowledge or this water. The God from the land of mystery has given this to us. When we worship Him, we must be grateful."

Nun praised his two eldest sons, who had returned on their own to move the timber from where it lay in the mineral water. They had carefully constructed shelters so the rain could not interrupt the drying process. All the sodden timber had fully dried.

As they talked, the sky darkened till it was nearly dark green in color. It was now the dry season, but that didn't mean it wouldn't rain. The wind came up, and the huge dark clouds seemed to want to tear this little family off the ground and swallow them up. There was not going to be any salt making today. Quickly, all the family rushed to ensure that their cooking firewood was protected from the storm. Rain continued through the night.

The next day dawned with rain still falling heavily. Piari had no thought of using his bow and arrows this morning. He just wanted to squat in front of the fire and try to keep warm. But no matter how cold or wet, Nun and his family had work to do.

"We could be here longer than we expected if this rain keeps up," said Nun. "We must collect more firewood for keeping warm and for cooking. Look for the driest you can find, such as under rock overhangs."

Titam gave each family member a large banana leaf that she had cut down earlier. They all knew what to do with this, and it was a welcome relief. They turned the leaf upside down and placed the end over their heads with the length down over their backs. The raincoat worked well!

Late in the day the rain eased. By sunset the sky was clear, and a deep cold fell on the family. But their excitement anticipating the next day's activities, as well as the warm fire in front of them, held back any discomfort.

Mother and Sanison had cooked *kaukau* in the red-hot embers. "Yum! I love this hot, freshly cooked *kaukau,* Mother," said Piari. Titam smiled. Everyone else was too busy with full mouths to say anything.

Darkness crept in on the family as they enjoyed their simple but healthy food. Nun and Titam shared stories that taught life lessons and that illustrated the cultural values that must be passed from generation to generation. The night sky now blazed with light from the stars and galaxies above.

The next morning both Nun and Titam showed the children how to burn the timber that now had the mineral from the spring within its every fiber. It was important not to make too hot a fire.

Out of the corner of his eye, Piari saw a bird of paradise with its prized iridescent feathers. He raced over to his bow and grabbed a blunt-ended arrow. But as quick as Piari was, he was swung around by a strong hand that had grabbed his arm. "Piari, it is time to work. You can do this while waiting for the timber to burn, but for now you must listen and begin work." Father had spoken, and Piari knew there was no point in arguing.

Things went well for the rest of the day, and by night the combined mineral ash left over was scraped onto a bark plate. Nun and Titam were ecstatic. But each of the four children stared in disappointment.

The Fighter

"Where has it all gone, Mother?" asked Piapin. The older children were glad he had asked because the same question had sprouted in their minds.

"Surely you don't think that something valuable comes easy, do you?" Titam queried.

Nun cut in, "We will have to burn every piece of the timber and ensure we carefully keep all the ash before we can finally form a cake of bush salt."

The night had been clear and very cold. Darkness was just beginning to give way to light. The moon still threw a strong glow through the trees. The family awoke to a beautiful sound. Was that singing?

Sanison touched Titam's arm and asked, "What is that, Mother?" Titam knew the sound instantly. She was strangely relaxed and even glad. "The *taia kali* are honoring our family with their presence, Sanison."

The boys were more anxious. Piari whispered to his father, "I didn't bring the fighting arrows as you said. But I should have!"

"Relax, son," Nun said softly. "It is the *taia kali*. They are from God of the land of mystery. They have nothing bad in them. They are our friends."

The sight before the family was a truly beautiful one. These special beings looked like men but had wings and were clothed in soft white light. They walked gently among the branches up in the tall tree beside the bush camp.

Nun quietly gathered his family together and explained to them about God, the Creator of all things.

"Is He old, Father?" asked Piapin.

"Yes. Very old. But He will never die. He lives forever. His strength remains with Him always."

As the morning light gained intensity, the *taia kali,* with their soft music, slowly moved on. The children, even Piari, could have stayed there all day. There was a peace that seemed unique to this experience.

But there was still much to do in making the bush salt. There would be three more days of making ash before they would have enough salt to shape into a large cake that could be used in trade—plus a little, of course, for sharing with the village.

With the prized cake of bush salt in hand—in Titam's *billum,* that is—the family cleaned up the campsite and began the journey back to Niungu. The children were excited to get back and share with their friends all that they had experienced. It was not often that village people traveled far.

Having slept on the trail overnight, the family finally trudged wearily into their home village very late the next night. A couple of dogs made a half-hearted attempt at barking. The air was cold, and they kept curled up to keep warm.

Nun and his two older sons stumbled to the *manhaus* to sleep, immediately benefiting from the warm fire inside. Not noticing the thick smoky air, they were after the warmth. One or two greeted them, but the storytelling could wait for another night.

Titam, Sanison, and young Piapin were facing the likelihood of a cold hut with no fire. This would mean some time to get a fire going so they could keep warm. But the wife of Nun's cousin saw the family arrive and made her hut available. They could share space tonight. Hospitality was the Engan way.

Fact File

The island of New Guinea has thirty-seven of the world's forty-one species of the Paradisaeidae family of birds.

Kumul, the common name used in Papua New Guinea for birds of paradise, played an important role in the social and cultural activities of Engan tribes.

The Raggiana bird of paradise is the national symbol of Papua New Guinea and is depicted on the national flag.

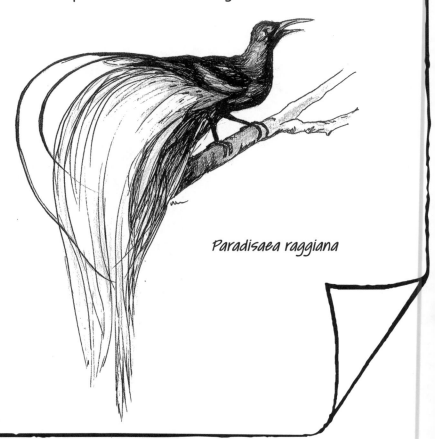

Paradisaea raggiana

Piari proudly showed Nala and his other friend Taop the bird of paradise he had shot while away with his family. His father had given him some time to hunt after all. "Father showed me how to gut the bird so it can dry. I'll look cool with this added to my headwear at the *singsing,*" Piari excitedly explained.

All the children had much to share with their friends this first morning back. All too soon, though, everyone had to begin their daily tasks. Nevertheless, lots of chatting was going on as gardens were tended and timber split.

The sun had reached the top of its cycle in the sky and had begun its descent into the afternoon when the world, as these isolated Engan people knew it, was changed forever. Some women tending gardens on the upper eastern edge of the valley began screaming and running. As the men heard the confusion, they raced to protect their women and children. The normal, well-organized daily grind of life suddenly exploded into confusion. Fear struck the hearts of both women and men as they watched a group of strangers make their way up the winding pathway toward the village. What was this? It looked like a person—but he was white!

Piari and Kainkali, along with other warriors, each nimbly strung an arrow to his bow. But some, including Nun, began to exclaim, *"Taia kali!"* Was this one of the *taia kali,* a being from the land of mystery? If it was, it had lots of black *taia kali* with it.

The white being spoke, but with words that no one could understand. And some of the black beings used words between themselves that sounded different again. Confusion reigned. The women hid in or behind the houses.

A small girl was more amused than scared. She giggled and asked her friend, "Is this a man or a lady? The voice sounds like a man, but he does not have big hair like that of a man."

"And look at those lips," a boy pointed. "They are not like ours. They are so small!" And he laughed with all his might.

Then one of the group who looked similar to the people of the Piapri tribe spoke in their own language. He explained that this was a white man and that he represented the government. *What is a government?* Piari and many others kept their arrows strung with bows taut, ready to kill these intruders if they showed any hostility.

The black men pointed long sticks at the warriors as the translator passed on the message from the white man. "My name is Jim Taylor. I have been sent by the government to find the people who live in these mountains. Put down your weapons. We are not your enemy."

Pakau called out, "Keep vigilant, men. This could be a ruse to have us off guard and then kill us." The translator heard this and encouraged the warriors to put down their weapons. "The government is a friend of the people. It will try to help all the people."

By now the warriors' arms were getting very tired. It takes much strength to pull back a black palm bow—let alone hold it in position.

While most children hid behind their mothers in fear of this weird human being with white skin, one brazen young boy moved toward him. Who was that? "Piapin, come here," Titam called fearfully. But Piapin was on a mission. He just had to know—was this really a man? He slowly stepped up to Jim Taylor and reached out, something everyone else wanted to do. He touched Jim Taylor's leg. It felt like a human leg, but he rubbed the side of it just to be sure. Jim Taylor let out a hearty laugh and bent down to shake the inquisitive boy's hand.

This was too much for Piapin. He shot away back to his mother in an instant. But the ice had been broken, and the tension eased between the black men pointing the sticks and the warriors holding the bows and arrows. Piapin excitedly and proudly reported to everyone that while the man's color was that of the *taia kali,* this could be just a man with white skin and straight, light-colored hair under his funny hat.

The translator continued passing on Jim Taylor's message. He said that the policemen with him had weapons called guns and that they are stronger than any spear or bow and arrow. Piari was not alone in thinking this to be a stretch of the truth. Jim Taylor called three policemen forward and had them aim their guns away from the people but at some casuarina trees nearby. "Ready! Fire!" he yelled. Immediately, a loud, sharp noise came from the sticks. Women screamed. Men, normally brave and fierce warriors, ran in the opposite direction. Some, including Piari, stood firm but were terrified.

Then it dawned on everyone that the noise was nothing compared to the damage those sticks caused the trees. The bark and even wood was splintered. *How did they do that with those sticks, without even moving?*

Jim Taylor certainly had everyone's attention now. Much of what this government explorer said did not make sense to this isolated tribal group. But one thing he said resonated with Nun: "Tribal warfare is not good. There are other ways of resolving conflict. The government says you are not to engage in tribal fighting. If someone from another tribe rapes someone or steals your pigs or burns your houses, ask the government for help. The government will catch the people who do wrong and will punish them. It is not good to kill each other."

He then gave an order. Policemen pointed those powerful sticks called guns at Piari, Kainkali, and the other warriors. Then other policemen stepped forward and took the warriors' arrows. They took spears as well and gave them all to Jim Taylor.

"You are to stop your tribal fighting," he said sternly and then broke every arrow and spear. Piari was angry but did not move. Considering what they did to the trees, those guns would do serious damage to a man. Nun was impressed. The law of the government sounded much like the law of God handed down from the ancestors.

The translator asked whether the village would share food with Jim Taylor, the police, and the carriers. It was agreed that food would be cooked and that they could spend the night in the village. Then Jim Taylor opened one of the boxes that had been brought in by one of the black carriers. He lifted out a tool that looked something like a stone axe. He invited the men to come and look at it and feel it.

"It is used to cut wood," he said. "Is there a tree here that someone would like to chop down for firewood? One of my men will chop it down for you." Nun pointed with his chin to a tree not too distant but far enough from the huts so as to be safe.

Piari nudged Nala and Taop, and with a smirk whispered, "This'll be fun to watch—one man trying to cut down a tree by himself." Most others thought the same. *How long is this white man planning to stay around? It will take two men a full day to chop down that tree.*

One of the policemen took this shiny and flat axe from the white man and walked over to the tree. He began swinging and cutting. The whole village looked on in wonderment. The buzz of surprise and discussion was loud.

This axe made huge cuts at every blow. After several minutes, there was a creaking sound, and the top of the casuarina tree began to move. A few better placed blows and that tall tree came crashing down. There was shocked silence followed by exuberance. Jim Taylor called for quiet. He said that these axes would come to this valley when the government comes.

Sleep did not come easy for anyone that night. Never before had they seen a white man. Never before had they seen such powerful weapons. Never before had they heard of a government. And never before had they seen an axe like that!

Jim Taylor and his team left the next morning, heading farther west. Life returned to normal after the excitement of that visit settled. There were no more visits by white men. This promised "government" did not come—at least not for a couple more years. But this visit indicated that change was coming.

Piari was not happy about his broken arrows. And this talk of stopping tribal fighting? Foolishness!

Fact File

The first time the people of the central western valleys had direct contact with the outside world was when Jim Taylor led an overland expedition from the Sepik River to Mount Hagen in 1938.

Jim was an officer of the Australian administration. He eventually married locally and made Papua New Guinea his home.

His daughter, Meg, was the Papua New Guinea ambassador to the United States, Canada, and Mexico from 1989 to 1994.

Chapter Seven

Sleep is fitful during the cold nights in this high mountain region. Woven bamboo mats on the dirt floor of the hut help alleviate the cold a little. A bark cloth wrapped as tightly as possible around the upper torso also helps keep the cold mountain climate from seeping through to the bones of children and adults alike. The evening starts with a subdued but very warm fire in the middle of the hut. Over the hours, this transforms into glowing red embers. And as the night wears on, these go dark, and the cold weighs heavily on all.

Titam and the other women reignited the cooking fires early in the morning, as they did every morning. Piari and his brothers stirred from their sleep. They were used to the thick smoke hanging in the air as it tried to press its way through the grass roof. But the smell of food cooking nearby? *Mmmm!*

As the boys emerged into the cold, crisp early morning, they saw, as usual, the many "smoking" huts nestled among gardens and trees that dripped with the damp of morning dew. This morning some boys and girls had already built separate small fires and were huddled around them to keep warm.

"*YonGAM*-oooo" (good morning), Nala wearily called, still half asleep.

Rubbing his eyes, Piari robotically responded, "*YonGAM*." The children stood around and quietly chatted. But this was soon interrupted as mothers gathered their families to eat. Then both mother and father would set out the family work plan for the day.

The girls and very young boys would make their way to the gardens some distance from the huts. Life depended on those gardens. It took twelve months for the staple food, *kaukau,* to grow and mature at this altitude. So the women and children had to plant rotational crops, constantly tending them so that there would always be food for the family.

The men and the maturing boys would all pitch in with the women and children when it was time to make a new garden. Indeed, the whole village would join together to help a family clear the land and turn over the soil for the first time.

But today there were other matters for the men. Tribal fighting had been going

on for some time, and with the killing of the fight leader the previous day, it was felt that it may be time to bring this current fight to an end. As the morning sun began to bring warmth into the air, it found the men of the village seated cross-legged in a circle on the bare ground. The young men sat as close as they dared but clearly behind the senior men. Piari, as famed a warrior as he was, was still young and knew his place. He sat behind with his friends.

A *bigman* spoke. "The tradition in our valley is to bring the fighting to an end with a compensation ceremony. Last night we all heard the echoing message down the valley that we succeeded in killing the Aowl tribe's fight leader. Now we have made it clear that we are a strong tribe with honor. Are we ready for an end to the fighting?" There was a murmuring of assent from the gathering, Nun included.

At this critical moment, something happened that had never happened before. A noise—what was it? "A flash flood!" someone shouted. Their blood ran cold with immediate fear. It sounded like the catastrophic floods that had killed people in the narrow gorges on the mountainsides. One or two began running and shouting to the women and children in the gardens. But they were halted by others shouting out to listen again.

It seemed to be coming from high up in the sky. All the men looked up. The women and children in the gardens looked up too. What was that? A bird? A huge and noisy bird? Piari had never seen anything like it. No one had! Was it really a bird or something from the land of mystery that Nun often spoke about?

Piari and a couple of other warriors instinctively placed an arrow to the string of

The Fighter

their bows and shot high into the sky. But this pathetic effort revealed how high up the "bird" really was. It was foolishness to try to shoot whatever it was with an arrow.

Then, as quickly as it appeared, it moved out of sight and then out of hearing. There was much discussion about this phenomenon. Some said it was a sign—but of what?

Nala's father, Pakau, called everyone together again. "This is an omen. We must not stop this fight with the Aowl too quickly. When we want to take off our beards," he continued, "we have to pluck each hair out, one at a time. It really hurts. Only when we have pulled out every hair do we put hot mud on our faces, followed by hot water to soothe the pain."

Pakau was telling a story, the Engan way of making a point. He did not believe that it was time to stop fighting. He believed that they should not stop until they had completed the task of making the other tribe suffer for having stolen those pigs. Only when the enemy feels the pain will they think twice before doing such a thing again. "Our pigs are central to our economic and ceremonial lives. Who knows whether they will come back in seven days and steal more pigs. We cannot afford to appear weak!" Pakau's large human hair wig extending widely on each side of his head, and his charcoal-blackened face added weight to his point.

"We all know the laws of our ancestors." It was Nun's turn to talk. "As tribal leaders, we call on our women and children to observe these essential laws. What are these laws? The first is: *He who would seek favor of God must not murder without weighty cause.* While stealing our pigs is a bad thing, it is not a reason to kill. One of the enemy is now dead. We have already broken the law. How much more do you want to go against the law of our ancestors?"

The senior *big man* invited others to speak. Many defended the need to injure and, if need be, kill for the sake of the tribe's future security. It was a long meeting, because each man took the opportunity to make his point with a colorful oratory display. A decision, though, was finally made. The fight would continue—in two days' time.

The decision needed to be broadcast throughout the valley and beyond. One from the group was sent to the top of the ridge with the message. Once at the most strategic spot, he stood tall and held his arms up high with his hands clasped together so his lungs could draw in the maximum amount of air. "The fight will continue-*ooooooo*! We will fight on-*ooooooo*! We will fight again in two days' time-*ooooooooo*!" The echoing message, repeated again and again, bounced off the valley walls and over mountaintops. It was heard near and far. The enemy tribe certainly heard it loud and clear.

The men began to disperse. It was time for another very important tribal activity. Nun called Piari and his older brother to join him to split firewood—hard work with just a stone axe. "But Father, I need to check my arrows for the fight," Piari remonstrated.

"Oh, Amusa, why will you not listen to your father? There is a God in the land of mystery. He gave the law to our ancestors. Why will you not obey?"

Fact File

The terrain of Papua New Guinea is mostly rugged high mountains and coastal lowlands. Even the lowlands are often difficult to navigate because of swamps and/or limestone caverns.

In such terrain, the most viable means of transportation is the airplane. Aircraft were critical to opening Papua New Guinea to the outside world. They remain an essential means of travel and communication today.

An Adventist Aviation airplane

The *Andrew Stewart*, a Cessna 180B bought in 1964, was the first airplane bought by the Adventist Church.

Chapter Eight

Piari, I know you enjoy hunting. Please use your arrow-shooting skills to help prepare for our special elders' gathering today." Nun was the most respected elder in the tribe when it came to the ways of the ancestors. He was to lead out in a most sacred event this day. "Today we *gote mau piya pelyo*. And we will need some quality birds for this, as well as some quality *kaukau*."

While Piari was already a proven warrior, there were some activities he could not join because he had not yet gone through initiation. Nun wanted his son to think about deeper issues and prepare for manhood. His assistance in gathering a key part of the sacrifice might do something to kindle tribal values and a respect for God, he hoped. Pigs were never to be used for such a sacrifice. But the sacrifice did need to involve a creature that had blood running through its veins.

"Remember, Amusa, whatever you collect, it is to be a healthy creature," Nun called to his son as Piari set out. With bow and blunt-tipped arrows in hand, Piari made his way across the Lagaip River and into the highland forest in search of birds for sacrifice. These birds needed to be of the best quality. Two hours later, this maturing young lad had six birds in hand. His father was proud of him.

"Well done, Amusa. These birds will do perfectly. If you pluck them carefully, you can keep the best feathers for your headdress decorations."

The elders of the village had chosen who would go to the mountaintop that day to sacrifice to God. It was a most sacred occasion. And, as the law directed, that did not include any women or children. If anyone not chosen saw this event, they would have to be killed. Piari, his friends, and younger brother and sister were all intrigued by this secretive event. But they knew not to ask and to keep their distance.

With birds, *kaukau,* and taro in hand, along with firewood and a fire stick, the chosen men climbed the steep mountain to its summit. Once there, they built a fire and heated stones on the fire. They dug a hole and in it placed the hot stones, followed by the birds, and then the *kaukau* and taro wrapped in banana leaves.

45

The Fighter

The food was carefully laid out in sections. The underground oven, *mumu,* was complete when more hot stones were placed on top and sealed by more banana leaves, and finally, dirt packed tightly over it all.

While all this was happening at the top of the mountain, the rest of the village tried to carry on with their normal daily routine, such as gardening and cutting firewood. The women realized the significance of *gote mau piya pelyo.* But Piari and his friends did not. They enjoyed the games they created in the course of their tasks.

On the mountain, the elders had placed the sacrificial food into segments within the *mumu,* a segment for each elder from the various families in the village. When the normal cooking time was up, the food was taken out and placed on a mat of woven leaves on a carefully prepared and swept surface. Vine "ropes" were placed on each segment and draped toward the respective family leader. Sitting back at a distance, the elders watched in awe for any word from God. This was all very important because the clear message was that God had the power of life and death. All wanted to be sure that He would give ongoing life.

The elders would look for potential signs of trouble. Possibly some food was not properly cooked, or a crack showed in the ground, or an insect settled on a segment of the *mumu.* The rope from the section where such a sign came led to the head of the family that was the focus of some potential trouble. Someone could get sick or could be killed in a fight.

But the elders did not just look for negative signs. If there was some wood with white in it or if light-colored lichen would fall down onto a segment, then the message would be that the person would live until they are old, with white hair.

"Mother, Papa is coming. Papa is coming!" called Piari's sister. It was late in the day, and Sanison was the first to see her father coming. She trusted him and loved to show him things that she had found during the day. She ran to him, calling out, "Papa, look at this flower I found in—" But she stopped short. Things did not seem right. When she looked up into his face, her own dropped and she withdrew.

The message from God was not good news this day. Numerous cracks had formed over the segment of the *mumu* with the rope leading to Nun. They understood that this was serious. A sign also came to the segment of the *mumu* that led to Nun's brother. Maybe someone would get sick, be injured, or even die.

This was a troubling day indeed!

Fact File

While many traditional cultures within Papua New Guinea were animists—believing that all animals, dead ancestors, vegetables, and minerals have a spirit, thus giving them a supernatural aspect that can help or hurt—the Engan culture was very different.

The Engans had a cosmic perspective with three layers:

(1) the heavenly layer where the Creator God and taia kali lived, having no sinful urge whatsoever and being the source of blessing;

(2) the material world where humans, animals, and evil spirits live, having yama (the urge to sin);

(3) and the underworld, where the spirits of dead ancestors existed, who were neither good nor bad.

While this belief meant that there was no need to fear the evil spirits or the spirits of the ancestors, most still allowed superstition and fear to erode trust in the power and goodwill of God and the taia kali.

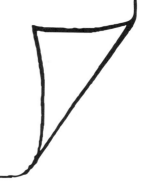

Chapter Nine

The next evening, the darkness of night settled quickly on the village as a fog also began to move into the valley. The cries of birds of paradise and the occasional barking of a dog was all that could be heard.

The men who were involved in the fight would have checked their weapons already. If they were to use bows and arrows, they would carefully check the black palm bow to ensure there was no cracking. They also examined the bamboo "rope" onto which the arrows were strung. They looked at each tie, as well as the condition of the bamboo. Enormous pressure was exerted on this bamboo as the bow was pulled back to its maximum so as to give speed and distance to the arrow. These arrows could hit a mark as far as 328 feet away (close to one hundred meters)!

If the warrior was planning to use a spear, then the full length—about six and a half feet (two meters)—had to be checked for any fault. Along with this was the elongated Engan shield. The three layers of bark, each with the grain turned in a different direction, made the shield a very effective protection against incoming arrows or spears.

With the weapons checked, the evening would normally call for stories—stories of fights and heroism, stories of tribal pride, stories of the past and of the future. This night, though, was different. There was an air of gloom about. Both men and women wondered about the events of the day.

The families had eaten in the *hauskuk*. The women and children would sleep there on the woven mats that lay around the fire on the bare ground. The men left to go to the *manhaus*. They could be seen in the fog-frosted moonlight moving quickly with arms crossed over their front and hands clasped on the opposite shoulder. This "highlands hug," which helps to maintain body warmth, is learned early in life. Ducking into their low hut, someone would lay a log on the fire to take them into sleep. Morning would come soon enough.

"*Arrrrrrggghhhh!*" The scream jarred the stillness of the night. "*Ip! Ip!*" (Come! Come!) A crescendo of excited voices came from outside. People quickly emerged to see four huts burning. Piari raced across the village toward his friend Nala's hut. It was already nearly destroyed.

"Is everyone out?" someone yelled.

"Yes, we are all safe," came the trembling response from Nala's mother.

Some men grabbed stone axes and spears and raced in the direction of the enemy tribe. This was surely the work of the Aowl tribe.

The fires soon became just a glowing oval shape in the dark night. It was certainly fortunate that everyone escaped injury. No babies were in those two huts; if there had been, it was likely they could not have been saved.

Nala's mother said to Titam, "All we have left are the earthenware pots. Everything else has been destroyed."

While possessions in a traditional Engan home were limited, they were of great value. The string bags, *billums,* used by the women to carry their babies, garden produce, and anything else that needs transportation—were woven from a string hand made from beaten bush fibers. These fine fibers were carefully prepared, then placed together and laboriously rubbed with the palm of the hand against the leg so as to bind them together into a long piece of string. A simple *billum* takes months of intensive work to make and is of great importance to life in the village.

The Fighter

Piari found Nala looking quite depressed. "That was too close, Piari. One of us could have been burned to death!" he said as his friend came to give support.

"We'll get them. The fight today will really be on. I'll pay them back for more than stealing pigs. I'll make them pay for burning down your hut, as well." Piari was worked up. He was angry. He meant every word.

Nun called out so all the village could hear. "The whole village will join together to build a new hut for each family affected by this terrible deed. You will be well cared for. We all know that the whole community looks out for each other."

Once the fight was over, the whole village did pitch in to help build new huts, cutting timber together, pulling *kunai* grass together, erecting the structure together, and weaving the walls together. And they did it with great gusto, singing and chanting as they worked. The bond of friendship between all families in the village was very strong indeed.

But for now, the immediate thought was revenge. Morning was not far from dawning, and there was no time to settle back into sleep. The warriors started small fires in the open area. They also began rubbing pig grease on themselves, earlier than normal. Their chanting grew as group after group built up their anticipation for the fight this day. Women also emerged earlier than normal. The whole village had been impacted, and everyone felt the extreme tension.

At this same time, Nun had confirmation of more trouble. He saw the *taia kali,* the winged beings who sang softly among the tree branches, fly away and leave the Niungu village. This was a bad omen!

Chapter Ten

The first light of day revealed a scene of horrific devastation. The enemy had dealt a heavy blow to the Niungu village. Yet, more trouble was in store for this close-knit community.

Younger children came out and, unaware of the significance of the previous evening's happenings, began playing. A couple of children moved away from the huts and were playing near the gardens. Dragging uprooted lengths of *kaukau* vine, they playfully raced back to where the men were standing around their fires.

"What are you doing?" shouted one young warrior. The others looked and gasped.

An older warrior angrily yelled, "Go find your mother. You are in serious trouble for spoiling the garden. You know you are not to pull food from the garden!"

"But we didn't," one of the children replied, fearful of the trouble that seemed imminent. Realizing that the children were not to blame after all, the men began running toward the gardens, fear and anger boiling hotter and hotter inside them. Arriving at the gardens, they saw that the enemy had attacked the essence of their subsistence by ransacking the plants. This had probably happened while the village was focused on the burning huts. Women and children joined the men, gazing upon the destruction.

Everyone knew that it would take twelve months for new crops of *kaukau* to grow. An old man mumbled to no one in particular, "Food's going to be scarce. We are going to be hungry."

When Piari's mother arrived, her heart sank. Theirs was one of the gardens affected. She began to cry out in the agonizing, shrill Engan way when one is grieving. "Not only the *kaukau*, but the cooking bananas? Look! Cut off at ground level. It will be a long time before we can eat from our own garden again!" All her hard work to provide food for her family was now to no avail. How would they eat? How would they survive? Other women came to console her. They would share their food with Nun's family. All would eat less so that no one went without. That was the law of the village. It was the Engan way.

The Fighter

Piari and Kainkali stepped up to their mother. "We will get revenge for this, Mother—for this, for the burning of the huts, and for the pride of our tribe!" Kainkali was not normally as hotheaded as Piari, but this had sent him over the edge.

Even Nun was moved to anger at this turn of events. In contrast to most in the village, he rarely ate pig because he always said that it was not good for you. "Food from the garden is what we need. That is what is good for you," he would tell his

children time and time again. And now their garden was destroyed!

The warriors of Niungu approached the fight that day angry and thirsty for revenge. The original cause of the fight had taken second place to this new aggression. Piari, as always, was right in the middle of it all. The warriors shooting arrows would go in front and fire volleys at the enemy line. There was lots of shouting—angry insults being hurled next to spears and arrows. Directions and orders to fellow warriors added to the cacophony: "Advance! Retreat! Advance!" And so the day wore on.

Fighting resumed the next day. But for an occasional small wound, neither side made any real headway. This continued into the third day.

Life in the village could not settle into a normal routine with all this tension and fighting.

"Mother, I am scared. I don't want to go to the garden today. Someone might come and kill me," Piapin whimpered.

While only Piapin voiced it openly, all were nervous. But they did venture into the gardens. Time was precious. The gardens had to be restored!

All pitched in and helped where the gardens had been destroyed. A huge amount of *kaukau* had been pulled out. There would be food to spare for a while as they ate that which had been pulled. But after that, there would be a serious shortage for a very long time to come.

As did the other women in their respective gardens, Titam bent over and built the ground up again into large mounds about three feet high (one meter) and six feet across (two meters). The children helped as best they could.

Once the mounds were rebuilt, it was time to replant. "Sanison? Piapin? You know what to do next. We have done this many times before. But we need to do a lot today, a lot more than we normally do in a day's planting. Bring me pieces of *kaukau* vine for planting from all that tangled mess the enemy has left." The children selected the best sections of vine and broke them off, taking them to their mother. Titam pushed the sections of *kaukau* vine into the sides of some mounds. With three helpers, it was not long before there were more sections of vine than needed. "That's enough, children. *Yakapalinooo!* [Thank you!]"

The children excitedly began helping Mother to plant, nearly forgetting the cause of this extra burden on a people whose very existence depended on producing gardens. All this backbreaking work went on and on.

"That's enough!" Mother called to her eager helpers.

"But, Mother, there are so many more mounds still needing to be planted," said Sanison.

"Yes, Sanison, that is true. But the other mounds will have to wait. We will need to plant again later. If we planted all the mounds at the same time, we would have lots of food at one time of the year and no food after that!"

Meanwhile, the fighting was going nowhere. But the warriors believed they had to keep face as a tribe. Both sides had to.

Then, a bloodcurdling cry of success arose from an opposing warrior. A kill? The rest of the Aowl warriors joined in as they saw that one of their warriors had successfully brought down a Niungu warrior.

The women back in the gardens heard the cry and shuddered. Was that their men calling out with ecstatic exuberance, or was it the enemy? The old men and those few who, along with Nun, disagreed with fighting, also looked in the direction of the fight and froze with fear. They looked at each other. Was this what God was telling them during the sacrifice on the mountaintop just a few days ago?

Piari knelt beside the fallen warrior. "Kainkali, you will be OK. We will get you back to the village." Blood was oozing from where the spear was still lodged in Kainkali's side.

A seasoned warrior came and broke off the long spear shaft but left the point embedded in Kainkali. *"Argghh!"* He screamed with the pain of this agonizing but essential act. Three warriors lifted Kainkali and carried him off, with Piari also at his side. Piari still held his bow and arrows in one hand as he tried to comfort his brother.

As Kainkali's bearers approached the village, the women began the shrill and eerie cry of grief. Nun and his wife raced to their son's side. Nun was devastated but not surprised. God had prepared him for this.

The fighting had ceased for the day. One group, the enemy, had returned to their village with joy. But the Niungu warriors had returned bloodied and discouraged. The wise old men of the village quickly rallied around Kainkali.

"Piari, build up a fire!"

"Boil water, quickly, Titam!"

"Get some mud and heat it in the earthenware pot."

The wailing continued to express solidarity and grief. What seemed like confusion was really a community working together to save a life.

An old man brought sharp bamboo knives. Piari looked at these rough tools and shuddered. But he knew that if Kainkali was to live, they would have to remove the spear without leaving particles of the shaft behind, which could get infected. The wound had to be opened up. Success for such bush surgery was known, but not often. There was no other option.

Kainkali was weakened by the loss of blood. Yet the pain was so severe as the bamboo cut into his flesh that he convulsed and screamed out in agony. After what seemed an eternity, the old man removed the spear shaft and began to clean the wound and to dress it. Leaves had been collected from the jungle while the operation was taking place. These were special leaves that were known as healing agents. Some were packed into the wound. Others were placed over the wound. Then the wound was carefully covered with larger leaves and bound with soft vines.

Nun held his son's hand. Kainkali was alive—at least for now. He looked over at his hotheaded warrior son, Piari. Were those tears in his son's eyes?

Chapter Eleven

Some days later, there was nervous tension in the village as the elders contemplated the message that had just arrived from the tribe they were currently fighting. That tribe was ready to put an end to the fight. If it was agreed to, this would mean all the past would be put behind them. If the compensation ceremony were completed, nothing that had transpired would be held against the other.

Even Nala's father, Pakau, the tribal fight leader, was now ready for a conclusion to the fighting. "It is time," he said. The rest of the elders were in agreement. While young Piari, the fighter, found great relish in the tribal warfare, he was glad to see this particular fight come to an end. Kainkali was alive but badly injured. Kainkali would not be able to cut down a tree, split firewood, or go hunting for a long time.

The date was set for the elders of the two tribes to meet. "There will need to be compensation for the damage and injuries to each side and, of course, the death in the Aowl tribe that has transpired during this fight. Plan for that," the *bigman* advised the family heads. This compensation would cost the Piapri tribe up to one hundred pigs, because of the death and injuries sustained by the Aowl. And the Aowl tribe would have to pay compensation for the serious injury to Kainkali and the destroyed houses and gardens.

Piari helped Kainkali prepare for the ceremony. Though Kainkali did not yet have a human hair wig, he would still appear as a strong and feared warrior with his charcoal-blackened face and his body glistening with pig grease. The bush bandage would need to remain, though, because the wound would easily tear open again with the simplest careless movement. Bright feathers were added to Kainkali's hair behind a headband braided from fresh young bark and possum fur by his younger sister, Sanison.

Piari, ever the aggressive warrior, was also determined to show the other tribe that he was not to be taken lightly. His long loincloth on the front, intricately woven by his mother, was made of bark rope interwoven with white possum fur. A wide plaited vine waistband held this up, and a *tanget* clung to his back. Modesty was high on the agenda for Engans.

Piari certainly did not want any shame for himself, either. He placed a straight pig bone through the hole in his nostril and smeared himself with pig grease. Then he decorated himself with colorful feathers, some of which he had recently collected. He placed each of his hands through an armband that had rats' and bats' claws woven into them and pushed them up around the top of each arm. And while his father would wear around his neck the recently acquired kina shell, Piari would wear on his forehead several rows of toea shells platted onto soft beaten bark.

Piari placed over his head a charm necklace of possum teeth. He knew his father did not approve of such things. "We are in God's hands," he would say. "We do not need sorcery and charms." But most in the village used these things, and Piari was not going to be different.

Finally, he placed his very own stone axe into his waistband. He did look the part!

Trying hard to be manly, Piari was still a boy at heart. It took all his and Nala's will to walk steadily with the rest of the village people as they made their way to the chosen ground. It was here that the compensation ceremony would be held.

He looked around. Many men carried long slim drums, the *kundu.* All the men and women—and even most children—were dressed up for this occasion. Bodies glistened with pig grease. The women, with painted faces, walked with pride in beaten golden reed skirts rustling to the knee in the front and a quantity of the same at the back nearly to the ground. Large and intricately designed *billums,* full with compensation gifts, hung back from the women's foreheads. Many pigs were led by a rope attached to a lower leg. Other larger pigs were tied to a pole between lengths of timber and carried upside down between two men.

The site for the meeting of the elders of the tribes was where their respective territories met. It was a clearing of some size so as to minimize fear or threat.

The men lined up, looking fearsome and grand as they began swaying to the beat of the *kundu.* The melodious and hollow tone of these uniquely traditional drums gave reasonable comfort to all involved. The chanting of the men and women grew in intensity. Pigs were passed over as compensation was debated and finally agreed upon.

As Nun looked on, he thought to himself, *If we had done this at the start, there would be no need to fight! God does not want us to fight. How can I help my tribe and my family to understand this?*

His thoughts were interrupted as he overheard his children talking together. "The payment of compensation has to be carefully thought out," Kainkali said to Piari, Piapin, and Sanison. "Once the compensation is agreed upon and payment

57

The Fighter

is made, there can be no return to the matter. We cannot think of that tribe as the enemy because of the past. All must be put behind us. Even I cannot hold my injury against this tribe once compensation is paid."

Nun was pleased. It was a glad moment in a bad time. *This is the way of our ancestors. This is what God from the land of mystery taught our ancestors,* he thought.

But Piari was thinking differently. Piari the fighter wanted revenge.

Fact File

Tribal fighting in the Enga Province often goes on for a week and can last a month or more. Members of one of the tribes can initiate an end to the fighting. Sometimes peacemakers from neighboring tribes might intervene, calling for an end to the fighting.

Animosity is not resolved until compensation, called tei, is paid. The amount is determined by the level of injury and damage. A death can cost between fifty and sixty pigs.

An initial peace offering is made with a pig that is killed and cooked and shared at that time. Then, months later, when they have had time to raise the number of pigs required for the tei, real compensation is paid in live animals.

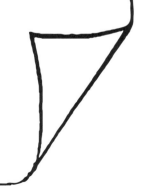

Chapter Twelve

We are going on a journey, Piari. Grab your weapons and stone axe. Say goodbye to your mother, brothers, and sister," Nun said one morning during the wet season. The ground was seeping with runoff, and clouds hung heavily over the twelve-thousand-foot mountains in the south.

There was a hint of mystery in Nun's voice, and Piari knew that something unusual was about to happen. The look in his mother's eyes convinced him to ask his father, "Is this my time?"

"Yes, son," Nun replied, smiling. "This is your time for initiation. This is to be your *shangai*."

Other young men were gathering with their fathers and the old men from the village. Piari noted that his friend and cousin, Nala Pakau, was there and was excited to also see his other great friend, Taop Talai, among them.

Walking up to his friends, Piari whispered, "Are you scared?"

"Sort of," Nala replied. Standing as tall as possible and flinging his chest out, he continued, "But this is our time to become men and to step up to the mark. I mean, I will be able to do business transactions of my own. I can own lots of pigs and marry many wives. I can now become a big man—a true *big* man!"

Piari had never seen this side of his friend before. He was impressed with his drive and ambition.

"What about you, Piari? What do you want for the future?" Taop asked.

"I plan to be the fight leader for our tribe," he replied. "I will defend the pride and future of our village. Businessmen like you can count on me to protect you and all our interests."

And so these young men, who had still to pass through their initiation, mapped out a prosperous and safe future for themselves and the Piapri tribe in a matter of minutes. Little did they know of what really lay before them and how very soon their world was to change dramatically. Little did they know that their limited world of a few valleys would expand into a world of a large island that was but a speck among oceans holding huge continents. Little did they know that their world where Nun talked about the God of their Engan ancestors would open up into a world where that God would become far better understood. Little did they know that Piari, the tribal warrior, would become a warrior of a different kind. But that was still in the future. Their journey was just beginning.

The driving rain seemed determined to drench and freeze these boys and their elders as they walked. Holding long and shiny dark-green banana leaves over their heads helped a little. From a distance they looked like a banana plantation on the move.

Well into the night the older men decided it was time to stop. Finding whatever cover they could, each one finally fell into a fitful sleep. While it was still dark, the leaders woke everyone. It was time to begin moving. As they walked, they would reach into their small *billum* for some precooked *kaukau* and taro that had been provided by caring mothers and wives.

The trail took the party along the raging Lagaip River and then over a mountain range. Nun took the opportunity to share more with his son.

"Amusa, there is a story from our ancestors that you need to know. A girl gave birth to a baby. God came and said, 'I will go and get some water. This water gives eternal life. I am going to get this water for the baby, and after he has had some, you can give him mother's milk.' After saying this, He left.

"Now, the baby was hungry and began to cry. And that cry grew louder and louder. The mother felt sorry for the baby, and so, instead of waiting for God to return with the water of life, she gave him some of her milk. She had been standing on top of the mountain, but when God came back, she hid.

"God shouted, '*Karabi-oooo?*' (Life?) But the woman did not answer.

"And so God cried out again, but this time saying, '*Kumabai-oooo?*' (Death?)

"Only then did the woman answer, 'Yes, Sir.'

"But the answer did not come quickly enough. It did not come when it should have. And when it did come, it was after giving the mother's milk against God's counsel. And the answer came in response to 'Do you want death?'

"So God emptied the container of water with eternal life in it and went back to the land of mystery.

"And so the outcome was, 'He will die!' Instead of having eternal life, we die.

"We did not have to experience a life of pain and death. It came about because our ancestors did not obey God and took too long to respond to God's invitation for life. They made the wrong choice.

"Piari, you are about to become a man. You will make choices. Will you choose to obey God or disobey him? Will you choose life or death? I plead with you to choose to obey God. Choose life!"

After two days of walking, they neared their destination, an isolated spot

The Fighter

nowhere near any place the boys had ever been before. The married men now stopped. They would go no farther. A senior bachelor, an unmarried man, now took over. He kept the sacred plant called *lepe* or bog iris. The leader took the initiates on to where they would camp. The boys were not aware at this time that the camp was in close proximity to the sacred plant.

A boundary was established. This was now *tambu*—off limits to everything other than the initiation ceremony. First, a shelter had to be built. The leader gave directions: "You four go and cut a small tree, and split it to place upright around the walls.

"You two go and cut saplings for the roof frame.

"You two go and cut vines for holding the timber frames together.

"The rest of you, come with me, and we will cut *kunai* grass for the roof."

And so the group, already tired from the journey, began a long day's work.

Piari's group was to chop down the tree. This was no small task for stone axes! Horrible blisters formed on their hands, but they continued. The boys tied soft vines around their hands to ease the pain. While two of the four initiates chopped, the other two sharpened their blunted stones. It took the whole day and into the night to cut the tree and split it into the required sections.

Midway through the next day, the shelter was complete. The leader was pleased with what the boys had done. But that was not the *shangai;* it was only preparation.

The boys wondered what was to happen next. Nala whispered to Piari, "Do you know what is going to happen?"

"No, Nala. And I don't dare ask. No one ever talks about *shangai*—not even Kainkali after he returned from his initiation."

Chapter Thirteen

Boys, move into the clearing that has been marked out," came the order from the senior bachelor, who was overseeing the initiation.

Unbeknown to the boys, during the night the leader had gone to the site of the sacred plant and collected enough for the ceremony. "I hold here *lepe*. This is not like any other plant. It is sacred. The God from the land of mystery gave this plant to us so as to pass on virtues such as discipline, self-control, power, competence, self-assurance, moral excellence, and bravery. It is through this sacred plant that you are cleansed. Only through this cleansing can you become a man."

One by one, each of the boys moved forward and smelled the *lepe*.

The leader then announced, "We leave first thing in the morning for your eyes to be washed under the waterfall on the other side of the valley. Now that you have smelled the sacred plant, your eyes are to be washed and therefore your mind is to be purified. Then you will be able to see, even when everything is dark around you."

The boys understood the *tokbokis,* the Engan parables. They would not necessarily have better physical sight at night, but they would now be able to understand things that would otherwise be hard to discern; they would have wisdom.

"If you see anything bad during this experience, then you will have to return and go through the washing again." This meant that if they saw something like human or animal feces, or if they accidentally saw a private part of someone else's body, they would be dirty and need washing again before passing on to the next stage of *shangai*. And if they saw another person, man or woman, not part of the initiation ceremony, they would have to kill that person.

The leader led the boys in the direction of the waterfall. Silence fell on the group as the significance of the event began to weigh heavily on all. There was much self-reflection as they trudged farther and farther up the steep mountainside, deeper into the tangled jungle.

Piari was thoughtful. The way of his ancestors was important. It told of where

The Fighter

he had come from, of who he was, and of his community. And, as his father constantly reminded him, the way of his ancestors linked humans with the God who created them. *What does it really mean to be a man? And who is God? What do I have to do with Him?*

A thorn tore at his arm as he pushed through the jungle. His thoughts had taken priority over attention to the harsh environment surrounding the little-used trail. But even the sharp sting and trickle of blood down his arm did not overpower his sense of awe as he contemplated what life was really all about.

Suddenly, that contemplative silence was broken by Pelen, one of the other initiates. "Can you hear it? Is that the waterfall?" The leader continued striding forward, ignoring the questions. The initiates' hearts raced.

Chatter stopped abruptly as they climbed up and around a huge vine-encrusted boulder. Looking up, they saw a volume of water cascading from a height of over nine feet (three meters). Ferns and moss covered this wide rock face in different shades of green. The leader jumped nimbly across some boulders and stopped at the base of a pandanus palm. Climbing onto the palm, he reached up and cut down a large leaf. Even a stone blade can achieve much quickly in the hands of a skilled person. He shaved the leaf away until there was just a gutter left.

He then climbed up to where the water came to the lip of the waterfall. The boys watched with wonderment. *What is he doing?*

He edged his way to the center, careful not to slip. There he wedged the leaf into the rock face. Water began to run down the pandanus leaf gutter until a small trickle fell to the waiting group nine feet (three meters) below.

So this is how we wash our eyes, thought Piari. But his immediate thoughts were confused by the actions of the man above. He did not come back down right away. Instead, he was doing something behind the boys' line of sight. Clearly, there was some serious activity going on up there. Ever so slowly, the widely dispersed waterfall began to ease. And the stream coming down from the pandanus leaf gutter increased until there was a strong torrent of water falling from the single source.

Every one of the boys began to feel very uneasy. The look on their faces indicated they all were thinking the same thing. *Surely I am not going to have to stand under that torrent with my eyes open. That would hurt!*

All this time, no words were spoken. Once the leader came down from the top of the waterfall, he went to the pandanus palm and began breaking nuts from it. Continuing in silence, he chopped the sharp hook from each nut, two for each initiate.

"Your purification must be thorough," the leader finally said. "Your life and that of the tribe is dependent on your being fully clean. The God from the land of mystery can give you sight only if you are pure." Piari thought of his father, Nun, as he heard these words.

Then the leader began prying open each of the boys' eyes, placing the hooks from the nuts so that they remained open. The boys tried to be tough. They *had* to be tough. They were being initiated into manhood. Each boy had to walk under the torrent of water, head held up so that the water directly fell on the eyes. Cleansing could not come without agonizing pain.

After five washings, each boy stood silently nursing his pain but also reflecting on the meaning of this extraordinary event.

Time seemed to stand still in all this. So Piari couldn't be sure how long it was before the senior bachelor began leading the way back to the camp. Again, there was silence as they carefully descended the mountain and pushed through thick branches covered in green leaves. The boys' minds were going over the initiation ceremony. They recalled the warning that they were not to see anything bad. Where do you look when you don't want to see anything bad? "Don't look down, Piari, in case you see a pig's droppings!" yelled one of the boys. Most chuckled nervously.

Halfway back to the *tambu* ground, Takapin, one of the initiates, was in the lead. All of a sudden, he pulled his *tanget* leaves from his vine belt and there, before all the boys' eyes, were his naked buttocks! A groan rose from all the boys. "Oh no, Takapin! You're crazy! Thanks for nothing! We'll get you for this!"

All of them, except for Takapin himself, had to make their way back to the waterfall where, again, the leader pried open their eyes so they could wash five times. They were about finished when a sheepish Takapin appeared. "I was waiting for you all, bored and wandering around, when my eyes saw the droppings of a *muruk*."

"Ha ha haaa!" The boys laughed, enjoying this dose of justice for the clown. "Now we will wait for you, Takapin, while you wash your eyes again five times!"

It was quite dark by the time this now very reflective entourage finally made it back to the *tambu* ground. The leader declared, "You have smelled the sacred bulrush and now have been purified so you can truly see. You are now an adult.

"Now that you are adults, you have to be able to care for yourselves," he said sternly. "For the next five days, you will get your own food. And you are to do this only at night."

He explained to the boys much of what they already understood about life in the community: the roles of the men, women, and children. There were some new matters that they did not yet fully understand, though. One such matter was marriage. "There will be times in married life when the wife is not allowed to cook,"

The Fighter

he explained. "This will occur on a regular basis—for seven days in every four lots of seven days. It will also be the case for two weeks after the mother has given birth. At these times the man must cook. The husband and wife can eat together, but the wife cannot touch anyone or anything."

And thus began manhood. For five days they fended for themselves. Most of these young men ate well, having been successful in their search for food during the night. When they were not successful, the next day was long, and hunger haunted them.

Excitement mounted as the men—who were now all *men*—made their way to where their fathers and other senior men from the village waited. There they joined together for a *singsing*, an Engan dance. They moved in unison as they swayed and stepped forward and backward, chanting to the rhythm of the *kundu*. The older men, with their human hair wigs of various shapes, looked proud as they included these newly initiated men in the *singsing*. But the young men looked even more proud.

The experience had inspired deep thinking in each young man's mind. As they began the long walk back to the village, sunlight glistening on the sweating dark bodies, Nala thought of how he would succeed in trade, own many pigs, have many wives, and become powerful while still young. And Piari? This short but strong young man walked tall. He, too, had been forced to think about deep and eternal things. But his most prominent thought was that he was closer to his dream of being the fight leader for his people!

Chapter Fourteen

We're in serious trouble—all of us—the whole village!" Piari declared to his family. He and his father had just returned from sacrificing to God. It had not been a long time since Piari's initiation, and Nun felt it important now for his second-born son to experience this sacred happening. Maybe a close encounter with God would make a difference to his son who loved fighting so much!

Piari was clearly moved by the experience—especially the unexpected that had happened.

Engans know how to cook. They know instinctively when it is the right time to take the food out of the *mumu* so that it is cooked just right. Yet on the occasion of this sacrifice, all the food in the sacrificial *mumu* had not been properly cooked. This had never happened before! Of what was this an omen?

At seventy-two hundred feet above sea level, the high-altitude climate was most invigorating, with cool to warm days and cool to very cold evenings. There were just two seasons that marked the annual cycle of time, wet season and dry season. The dry season was the colder period of the year, as the lack of moisture in the air and clear nights brought the temperature down considerably. The start of this particular dry season was no different.

But then, for several nights, the temperatures plummeted much lower than normal. Severe frosts blanketed a large region of Enga. Not only was the Niungu village impacted, but so was the whole eastern Lagaip Valley and several valleys to the north and south. A week later, the unusual cold resulted in more severe frosts.

Titam, normally a strong woman both physically and emotionally, now showed fear in her eyes. "We are only just surviving now after the destruction of our gardens by the Aowl. Now this? People are going to starve. People are going to die!" Her words brought a shudder of fear upon all the children.

Nun agreed. "Our extended family, and the others who have so thoughtfully helped us, have themselves now lost all their gardens. This is truly a disaster!"

The survival of a subsistence culture is completely dependent on the garden.

The Fighter

No garden means no food. No food means starvation—that is, unless the wider community steps in to assist. But this was not possible now. Everyone was in trouble.

Sanison exclaimed, "Mother, all the plants in the garden look as if somebody has put fire to them. They look like they have been burned."

"Yes, Sanison. Frost is a terrible thing. It freezes the plants, and they immediately die and go black, looking like they have been burned." Titam continued, "Once we have eaten all the food that is now in the ground, there will be nothing left. We will have to go into the jungle and find food there. But so will everyone else in the village and in neighboring villages. There won't be enough for everyone."

One option was to trade with other villagers farther away who had spare food. But as the cry went from mountaintop to mountaintop in the traditional Engan way, it was clear that no village was spared from this disaster. The message from God to the Niungu people, noted by Piari at the *gote mau piya pelyo,* the sacrifice to God, was true.

Over the next few days, the village *bigmen* tried to find a solution. "Does any elder have suggestions of what we can do?" asked one of the more respected men.

"The jungle will provide survival rations for some. But it certainly will not be able to sustain the whole village until our gardens grow again," said one. "And it is not the time of the *karuka* nut, the fruit of the palm that grows high up in the mountains. Otherwise, that rich food may have helped," said another.

Nun spoke up. "Some of us who have married into other tribes will have to move our families to those other areas for a period of time." He paused for a moment, realizing the terrible impact this would have on the close-knit Niungu community. "I will try to find out whether Titam's home village has been affected or not." A few other men who had married from more distant tribes agreed to do the same.

Nun went to discuss the decision with his family. "Piari, you are to walk to your mother's home village in Yakananda. Find out whether that valley has been affected by the frost," Nun directed. Some of the precious food was prepared for Piari's two-day journey in search of his mother's tribe. En route, he would supplement this prepared food with some jungle food. Various gifts were also prepared. One such gift was a large *billum* that Titam had woven using string into which she had included large amounts of possum fur from the possum that Kainkali had caught when cutting the timber for the bush salt. When Piari saw this, his mind went back to that wonderful time when Kainkali was strong. But there was no time now for sentimentality. He stowed these items in his *billum* and set out east.

This was not the first time Piari had ventured east. In his sixteen or so years of life, there had been a couple of visits to his mother's home village. But this was under extreme circumstances. What would he find? Had the frost destroyed their gardens, as well?

The journey took Piari across very high-altitude country, an area that was normally much colder than his own home. During the day he kept warm by walking quickly. But the nights felt even colder than normal. He was used to keeping warm inside the *manhaus,* with the grass thatched roof causing the smoke, and with it the warmth, to linger. Out here in the open there was no such warmth, just the immediate heat from his fire. The rest of his body froze, alleviated a little by the pandanus leaves Piari tried to pack around himself.

Piari descended into the upper Wabag Valley. With relief he noted that this region had not been so severely affected by the frost. His heart lifted. It was possible that the family would survive this crisis after all.

His cousins, aunts, and uncles greeted him enthusiastically. As they listened to Piari tell of the disaster farther west in his inimitable Engan style, there was never any option. Of course their village would welcome them. Titam's family was their family. Nun and his family would be given land for a garden, along with food until that garden produced. The whole village would join together in building a shelter for them.

But Piari learned more than just the significance of blood relations on this trip. "Have you seen the white man yet?" his cousins quizzed him.

"Yes! Why? Have you seen one, too?"

"There are lots of them down the valley. They are preparing a place for their friends and a place for the monster birds to land," his young cousin Kojini interjected.

The Australian government had sent a district officer, local policemen, and engineers. A small government station had been established at Wabag, and work had commenced on an airstrip.

"I have seen just one white man," Piari continued. "He came out of the jungle a couple of seasons ago. We got such a surprise! My father first thought he was *taia kali,* an angel from God in the land of mystery. And he had a lot of black angels with him." As he recounted this first meeting with a white man, Piari laughed. "The little children initially ran away and hid among the trees. And the women hid in the huts. I strung an arrow to my bow. The black angels had weird-looking sticks they carried like weapons. But if they made any trouble, they would die swiftly at our hands.

"Eventually, once it was clear that this angel and the black angels with him did not mean any harm, the whole village came around to look at him. One of the young boys yelled out, 'Does he go to the toilet?' We all laughed, but we actually didn't know! The women and children started to come closer."

"Did you see how their weapons work?" Lamu, a cousin of similar age to Piari, asked.

"After we worked out that the man's name was Jim Taylor, he showed us how they worked. Wow! I thought that if they made trouble I could kill one or two. But at the order of the white man, the black men pointed their sticks at a tree. *Bang! Whack!* A huge noise and holes were made in the tree, but we didn't see what made the holes. Jim Taylor went to the tree and showed us small stones."

"The white man calls those weapons 'guns,'" Lamu said. "Did you get scared?"

"Me? Scared? No way!" Piari retorted. But the truth was that he and every Niungu warrior had a real fright. They would later see what terrible violence that gun could cause!

Piari's report to his family at Niungu was a great relief to all. As a family, they would immediately leave their home and move to Yakananda. Nun became ill just before they set off. But he and Titam knew that every day they hesitated, the food shortage grew more serious. Delay was not an option.

The family carried all their earthly possessions with them, which was not much. Sanison and Piapin had the task of dragging a pig with a bush rope attached to the pig's front leg.

"Father, let me carry your *billum*," Piari said to Nun as they walked along the rugged mountain track. He could see that his father was struggling. The air was bitterly cold at ten thousand feet above sea level. Though still struggling with the effects of the spearing injury, Kainkali took his father's bow and arrows for him.

Soon Nun began struggling to breathe. The family stopped. The older boys got timber together and built a bush shelter while Titam, Sanison, and Piapin collected firewood. Titam put her skills to work with her fire stick, and soon a fire was warming the little family. Titam and Sanison went in search of jungle food. Each of the family took turns watching over Nun. Those not on watch dropped in and out of fitful sleep throughout the night.

A loud, high-pitched cry woke the children with a start. Titam was holding the head of Nun in her arms, rocking backwards and forwards. Sanison joined her mother in crying loud and mournfully. Piari and his brothers sat transfixed. This was not a time to talk.

Anyone who heard that unmistakable cry would know that someone had died. After a long, excruciating silence, Titam sobbed, "With your father dead, what will we do?"

Kainkali took a long and hard look at Piari and Sanison, and said, "Don't worry, Mother. We will care for you." The three eldest would take responsibility.

"Kainkali is right. We will care for the family. We are both initiated. We are both men now," Piari said solemnly. Together the family mourned loudly.

Piari thought, *Is this all there is? What happens now to my father? If only I could ask him. He would know. He taught me so much about the ways and teachings of my ancestors.*

It was true. Nun had taught his son much. But it was equally true that Piari had not accepted much of it, just as most of the tribe had not. Might this be a turning point in Piari's life?

As the morning dawned, Kainkali and Piari prepared a bush stretcher. They placed their father's body on it and, as a family, set out to complete their journey to Yakananda.

Fact File

In the normally habited areas of the Lagaip Valley, the maximum temperature ranges from 61 to 66 degrees Fahrenheit (16 to 18 degrees Celsius) and the minimum from 45 to 48 degrees Fahrenheit (7 to almost 9 degrees Celsius). The higher altitudes get much colder than that.

Clear night skies at altitudes higher than six thousand feet above sea level can cause the temperature to drop below 39 degrees Fahrenheit (close to 4 degrees Celsius), bringing on a ground frost. Normally, most village gardens can cope with this. But when the temperature drops even lower and is repeated a few times within weeks of each other, normal food sources are decimated.

Research confirms that the severe frost in 1940–1941 destroyed gardens throughout the Lagaip and Kandep Valleys and caused many deaths.

People who cannot find support elsewhere are driven to foods that are not normally eaten, such as wild yam, wild taro, fruit of various figs, and usually inedible ferns. As well as being unpalatable, they also can bring on indigestion and diarrhea. Thousands of people died of starvation and complications at this time.

Chapter Fifteen

The wail of the women at Nun's funeral continued for several days, until the formal grieving period had ended.

Piari chose to answer his questions about the other side of death with what his tribe believed—that Nun's spirit would continue on. This spirit would help or hinder, depending on whether it would be appeased or not. They would be careful about cutting firewood from specific areas, to avoid the trees in which the spirits lived. Food, such as birds and garden produce, would be placed in caves close to the burial grounds by a small group on behalf of the village, thus providing for all the ancestors. If only Piari had listened more seriously to his father, he would have concluded otherwise. But he allowed superstition to rule both his head and his heart.

Piari's fame as a young warrior had traveled far, and he was treated with great respect in Yakananda, his newly adopted home. He walked tall with his stone axe slung by his side and one hand holding his bow and a fistful of arrows.

After the grieving period, Piari approached his cousin Lamu. "I am going down the valley to see these white men. Do you want to come?"

"We will have to be careful and go around the territory of our traditional enemy tribe. But we are not fighting right now, so that is easier. Let's go," Lamu replied.

"Please do not go, Piari," Titam pled. "Farther east of my home are many more tribes, most not friendly."

"Oh, Mother, remember that I am a man now," Piari insisted.

"Yes—and a headstrong man who enjoys a fight," Titam said. She added, "You are a stranger in this country and do not have the protection of fellow warriors as you had at home."

"I will be careful. I promise." And so Piari and Lamu began their journey farther down the valley toward the place Lamu had talked about, where white men were building houses and a place for the big noisy bird to land.

As these young men followed the jungle path, Lamu was proud to walk beside his cousin with such a reputation as a warrior, even at this age. Piari, with adventure ever his goal, wondered what he would find farther down the valley.

"Look! A *muruk*!" Lamu whispered loudly. "Shoot it and we will eat well tonight." Lamu was hoping to see his cousin's skills firsthand. But this was not to be.

"No, Lamu. We have an adventure before us, and it does not include killing *muruk*. That would take time. Let's keep going." Piari sounded focused, and he was. But he also had great respect for the *muruk*. A friend in his home village had been knocked down, kicked in the chest, and gouged in the back by this large flightless bird. His injuries were not a pretty sight.

It became obvious when the boys were getting nearer to the white man's village. There were lots of noises unfamiliar to Piari. They slowed their pace, cautious of ambush or some other unexpected occurrence.

At the top of a ridge, there before them was a sight neither had seen before. White men and black men were everywhere, rushing from spot to spot doing things neither boy could comprehend. The boys ventured closer, holding their weapons close and ready to react to protect themselves if needed. But as they got closer, Piari relaxed his grip on his bow.

"Look at those white men, Lamu! They don't look strong like an Engan warrior," laughed Piari.

"And they have different colored hair that sits flat," said Lamu. Both boys laughed.

"What unusual dress they have—even some of the black men."

The bravado was really a front for both boys—especially Piari. He did not want his cousin to know how scared he was in this alien world into which they had ventured.

After some time observing from the traditional Engan crouched position, Piari and Lamu drew back as a black man strode toward their vantage point. "*Alamandiooo*. You boys want some work?" he asked. He spoke the same language as they did, but they did not recognize him. He continued, "You look real strong, and we need more men like you to help prepare the *ples balus*."

"What is a *ples balus*?" Piari tried to sound confident. But even the great young warrior was finding this a challenge.

"Sorry, boys," laughed the stranger. "You must have just come in from the bush. My name is Kamap. This is my home area, Wabag. The white men are preparing a place for the *balus* to land. They call that a *ples balus*. The *balus* is something that carries white men and black men as well as lots and lots of other things. It flies like a bird; but the white men made it, and they sit inside it and make it go where they want it to go. You make your arrow go through the air. But once it has left your bow, you don't have any more control. They made the *balus* to fly through the air too. But they made it big enough to sit inside and control it."

"Have you been inside a *balus*?" asked Piari, as his excitement with this new adventure increased.

Lamu was sure he wanted no part of this. "There is no way I am going to let something like a big bird take me up into the sky."

Smiling, the man said, "Oh, I have not asked you your names."

"I am Piari. This is my cousin, Lamu."

"Piari? Now that is quite a name. Fighter? Warrior? We don't want any trouble here, boy," Kamap said strongly.

"I am a hard worker," Piari quickly interjected. "Let us help."

Kamap explained, "It is my job to find laborers. You can join that group over there. At the end of the day, you will get some food and firewood. Come and see me when you have finished the job, and I will show you where you can sleep tonight."

Kamap led the way to a group of men clearing trees. "You won't need your stone axe here," he said. "We have the axe the white man has brought." Piari's mind went back to Jim Taylor. It would be fantastic to try one for himself!

Lamu lingered back. He was fearful of this new world. Piari was fearful, too, but the adrenaline rush drove him forward. Piari turned his head as he strode behind Kamap. "Come on, Lamu. Let's do this!"

Fact File

A patrol post was established near Wabag in the late 1930s. The Australian government began constructing an airstrip in the early 1940s.

World War II, while not directly affecting this region, brought a halt to the government program in Enga. The airstrip was finally completed in 1945.

Enga became a province when Papua New Guinea gained its independence in 1975. The population of the Enga Province is currently around five hundred thousand. Wabag is the provincial capital and has a population of fewer than five thousand.

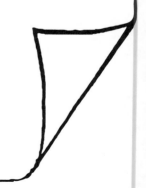

Chapter Sixteen

The rush and bustle of the white man's world was completely different for Piari and Lamu. Piari felt it was like being in the middle of a tribal fight all day every day. The boys worked hard for a couple of weeks and adjusted quickly to this unusual world, despite huge challenges.

One of those challenges was language. The white men spoke to each other in one language, and they spoke another language to the black men. There were plenty of locals, though, who spoke the language familiar to the boys. And there were black men who were not Engan. Some of these looked quite different, except for their hair, which was curly like that of the Engans. But all these black men spoke different languages with extremely unfamiliar sounds. This was very confusing. A common language was desperately needed, and it was called *pisin*. Necessity meant it did not take Piari and Lamu long to pick up what was being said.

Another challenge was the concept of government. Piari cringed as he remembered Jim Taylor mentioning this when breaking his arrows. The government was against tribal fighting. So while Piari was not happy, he certainly wanted to know what this government thing was all about.

He learned that Wabag was to be the village where the government lived. But the *bigmen* of this government had been sent by others from far away—from bigger *bigmen*. These men were in charge and gave directions. They had rules, or laws, that were openly talked about. Back in the villages, both Niungu and Yakananda, it was rare that laws were publicly declared. Everyone knew them because they were passed from father to son. It was only when one broke such laws that there was discussion on them.

But in this new world the *kiap*, the name given to the government administrator, seemed to make all the laws himself. Yet he kept saying that he did not make the laws, that they were the laws of the government. *This "government" thing is hard to understand,* thought Piari.

It would take some time for this concept to penetrate the minds and experience of a people who knew of only several valleys and who interacted only with the clans of their own tribe and with their extended family and neighbors. While Piari and his people were aware of tribes in the great beyond because of the trading process, it was not a world they ever needed to think about. The only sense of cooperation and mutual understanding was when a marriage took place between two people of different tribes. Piari's father was one of the brave men who took a bride from a different tribe.

Piari became fascinated by something that took place on the same day each week. White men went into a special house, and through the walls he could hear the sound of singing. This was nothing like the *singsing* he knew so well, but he liked it.

Black men also met together on the same day, but they met in the open. On one of these occasions, Piari made his way to where the black men were meeting. Their singing held him spellbound. Then he heard one of the men telling a story. It was a story that, while new, had a familiar ring to it.

Memories of his recently deceased father came flooding back to Piari. Nun had told and retold stories that had been passed on to him by his ancestors. These stories were of how the world began, of a great flood and fire that consumed all, of a baby born to a young woman who had not slept with any man, of laws that all should obey.

Piari had been too busy making bows, arrows, spears, and shields to take any interest in such things. Fighting was his all-consuming passion. Now he was hearing something similar to what his father had been saying. Something tugged at him inside. How was it that these people from a faraway place knew about the great personal God his father had talked about?

Mind you, some things were quite different—like the constant reference to someone they called Jesus—but the themes were the same. And so was the nagging feeling that he should listen. *Enough,* Piari told himself. *Father is dead.*

One day, Piari and Lamu were walking past a shed at the side of the *ples balus.* "What is that?" Lamu asked Piari with wide eyes. These houses were different from their village huts. They were tall, and you could stand up inside. Instead of *kunai* grass, they had something on their roofs that was shiny and hard.

The door was open and no one was inside. Lamu pointed with a jerk of his chin toward the open door. There was a box inside, and the boys could hear the sound of a man's voice coming from the box. The frizzy hair on both boys' heads nearly stood up straight for fear! They ran away as fast as they could and hid behind a tree to watch.

A white man gave directions to everyone working on the *ples balus;* they called him the foreman. He went inside the shed. The boys heard him and another man talking. But there was no one else in the shed before! They swallowed their fear and ventured close again—close enough to see inside the shed. Their skin prickled with fright again as they saw the foreman holding something in his hand and talking into it. Then, when he finished, the box spoke again.

"Is that a spirit?" Piari asked Lamu.

"I don't know, Piari. But I have had enough of this. Let's go back to the village," Lamu suggested. But just as they were beginning to move away, they heard a noise in the sky.

"Did you hear that?" asked Piari.

He didn't need Lamu to answer because the sound got louder. Both boys had heard it before, but from far away. But now it came toward them at low altitude. It was a *balus,* an aircraft. This is what Kamap had told them about. The boys were mesmerized with fear. Lamu just wanted out of there. But Piari stared, wide-eyed with wonderment, and decided that one day he would see one closer still.

The aircraft flew over Wabag to check the progress of the airstrip from the air. It turned several times, but this time it was coming so close to the ground that Piari and Lamu dove into the bushes, fearing it would get them. Others around them laughed, which did not go over well with proud Piari. They quickly got up again as the plane climbed back into the sky, making the strongest of noises.

It came back close to the ground two more times. Each time, things came out of the plane! They stared in amazement as the plane dropped bags of rice and other useful things. Another young man who was also seeing this for the first time raced out to catch one of these things falling from the sky, not realizing the weight and speed. He was hit by a bag of rice and lay there as if dead. Fortunately, he was not killed. But he lay unconscious for quite some time with a white man trying to help him. Eventually, he began moving again. Piari and Lamu realized they had to treat aircraft with respect!

This would be the last of such flights for more than a year because, unbeknownst to the two boys from isolated villages, the world was being torn apart by a tribal fight of global proportions that became known as World War II. The government put the airstrip construction on hold and called out of Wabag all but one of the white men and most of the black men. Piari, Lamu, and their tribes would hear and see many airplanes high up in the sky but, thankfully, this area would not experience the war firsthand.

Piari and Lamu made their way back to Yakananda, where family and village people waited fearfully, wondering what had become of these young men. "Oh, I have so much to tell you!" shouted Lamu as he raced into the village. Young and

The Fighter

old sat in a circle as the stories were told over and over again.

Titam looked at her son with mixed emotions. She was proud of her adventurous young man who showed such bravery, yet she also feared for him. She thought, *What is the difference between a brave warrior and a foolish warrior?*

Fact File

Life expectancy in the general population of Papua New Guinea is sixty-four years for men and sixty-nine years for women (as of 2014) but was much lower than this at the time of this story-possibly as low as forty to forty-five.

As a comparison, life expectancy in Australia is eighty-two; in Europe, it is eighty; and in the United States of America, it is seventy-eight. Life expectancy in many African nations ranges from fifty to sixty years of age.

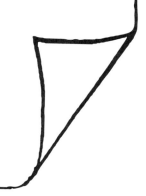

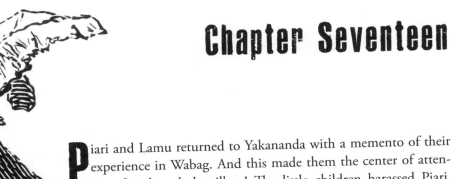

Chapter Seventeen

Piari and Lamu returned to Yakananda with a memento of their experience in Wabag. And this made them the center of attention for the whole village! The little children harassed Piari, "What is that? Is it a new stone axe? Is it? Is it?" The young boys were joined by the old men. Even the women, young and old, stared in wonder at the implement these two adventurers now wielded.

"The white men have brought these from their land. It is nothing like our stone axes," Piari declared with great authority.

"Lamu, let's show the village what it can do!" Lamu was excited and proud to be at center stage. Piari was used to it, but back in Niungu, it was always because of his fighting adventures.

The boys headed down the track to where the men had been cutting timber for constructing huts. Like a line of ants, the villagers trailed behind, each one eager not to be left behind and thus miss out on whatever this shiny new tool would do.

An elder showed Piari which tree needed felling next. Piari, ever one to make a point, said, "This tree is too small. Don't you have a large tree?" The men were surprised, and the women and children were amused. Someone pointed out a bigger tree, and Piari lifted the axe. He brought it back over his glistening muscular shoulder and swung it forward. The momentum of the axe increased as Piari brought all his power.

The old men cringed at this stupidity. They knew that unless the stone axe was handled with a delicate blend of sensitivity and strength, the bamboo binding that held the stone to the wooden handle would break and the stone would fly out. But as the axe head met the tree trunk, the village of Yakananda changed forever.

The villagers stared wide-eyed. Not only did the "stone" stay attached, but the axe sliced into the tree to a depth that no one had ever seen before. Piari had everyone's attention. With a gleeful smile, he yanked the axe from its tight hold in the trunk and took another swing. This time the blade of the axe came in under the previous cut. Out flew a huge wedge of the tree's flesh. The awestruck silence turned into a rabble of excited voices as young and old tried to come to terms with what they had just seen.

Lamu pleaded with Piari, "My turn, Piari!"

Reluctantly, Piari let Lamu take over with his axe. After several well-executed blows from Lamu, Piari took over again. In less than thirty minutes, the boys felled a tree that would normally take a team of men two days. In those two days, several stone axes would be used, having to be sharpened and resharpened. The old men reached out to hold this new axe that had such a strong and sharp stone. In amazement they passed this new axe from one to another, feeling it and turning it over and over. It was still sharp and in top condition.

After this exciting discovery, life at Yakananda began to fade into normalcy. Titam and her family fit in well in their adopted village. The daily routine supporting their existence continued: gardening, weaving, hunting, building, cutting timber, and chopping firewood.

The first dry season at Yakananda had come and gone, and now the wet season was nearing its end. It was hard to believe that a full year had passed since the family had moved to their adopted village.

One day Kainkali approached his mother. "It is time we returned to Niungu, Mother. The garden will be ready but overgrown with weeds. And we must be sure to hold claim to our land. Piari can now shave the hair from his face. He is older, and together he and I can care for you and the family."

He had been concerned for some time that their father's land must not be acquired by another. He and Piari had talked about this for some time. But Piari also had another reason to return home. He missed the fighting!

As they made plans for the trip, one morning Sanison came to Kainkali and Piari. "Mother is sick," she said. Other people had also fallen sick, and a few had even died. Piapin was scared. "Will Mother die, as the others?" he asked. "No. Mother is strong, Piapin," Sanison replied. But deep down, she, too, was scared. The plans for travel momentarily ceased. Mother would need to be strong for the journey back over the mountains.

But Titam weakened. After a few days, she called her children together. Her Yakananda family also sat around the fire inside the hut. She quietly said, "I am going to die." The boys stared wide-eyed. Titam continued, "You must return to Niungu. You must marry and bear children. Then our family will have a future." She looked at Piari and said, "Live a long life. Remember the teaching of your father."

Titam had never been the same since Nun died. Her strength had died with him. Now she had no more strength to fight this terrible sickness that had come to the valley. That very day she stopped breathing. The mourning cry was sounded again, as it would be for many others as a result of that influenza epidemic.

The Fighter

Men from the village helped Kainkali and Piari dig a large rectangular hole at the place of burial. Sanison blackened her face and wrapped the long string of gray mourning beads around and around and around her neck until they filled the space from her chin to her shoulders. There would be a period of mourning.

Sanison took over the woman's role in the family—cooking, gardening, and caring for her three brothers, especially young Piapin.

The need to return to their home village was now more intense than ever. But Piari's mind was swirling with grief and confusion. *Mother believed in God, as Father did. Father talked about a time in the future when good would come. But all this is not good.* The burning pain of his grief began to turn into anger.

Chapter Eighteen

An excited cry arose from the village as word spread that Nun's family was coming down the valley. But the mood turned somber and the wailing built to a crescendo as it became clear that both Nun and Titam were dead. Kainkali, Sanison, Piari, and Piapin were forced to go through another period of mourning as their extended family and village grieved.

The wet season had lingered in the eastern Lagaip Valley. The dark and damp roof of the family hut camouflaged its rotting state. But there was no doubt, long *kunai* grass had to be cut for a new roof. Piapin squeezed rich caramel-colored mud through his toes as he stood listening to his brothers and sister as they strategically planned for their immediate future. He was growing up fast. He needed to.

They made their way to the garden. "Oh, no!" Sanison cried. "It is much worse than I imagined." The bush had merged into the garden so thickly that if it weren't for the high mounds of dirt, it would not have been recognizable!

"Remember the Engan way, Sanison," said Piari. "Our village will work with us to fix the garden and the house. Come on, Kainkali, let's go talk to the men about this."

Piari and Kainkali left Sanison with Piapin and headed to where many of the men had gathered. In typical Engan fashion, they sat cross-legged with arms folded in front of their chests to keep in their body warmth. These two young men were just that—men, and they were respected as such. Piari was especially respected, as he had proven himself a fierce warrior.

"We will all go out tomorrow to cut *kunai* grass for your houses," said one of the *bigmen*. He continued in typical Engan oratory, "When the birds collect cobwebs and twigs for their nest, they do not just collect them and put them in a pile. No, they use them right away and make the nest." Both Piari and Kainkali knew they were not going to be given the meaning of the story. That was not the Engan way. They had to work that out for themselves. But that was easy on this occasion. The village would help not only with collecting the materials but also with fixing the houses.

The Fighter

The storyteller continued, "And the birds will not go hungry while they are building the nest . . ." The boys returned to the garden and explained to Sanison and Piapin that the whole village would work together to fix both the houses and the garden.

Piari took little time to get to the yearning of his heart. He pulled his uncle Pakau aside and said, "Uncle, is the pride and future of our tribe intact? It is no good if while I was away a cuckoo has sat on our nest."

His uncle knew just what Piari was asking. "The Aowl tribe continue to make trouble for us. Only one month ago one of our outlying gardens was raided. It was not destroyed, but all the *kaukau* was stripped from within the mounds, and the bananas were taken." Piari boiled inside.

He then found his friends, Nala and Taop. They shared together all that had happened since the destruction of the gardens that caused Nun and his family to leave.

Within two weeks there was a smart, light-colored new roof on both the *haus-kuk* and the general family house. Work was well underway to mend the high split-timber fence around the family houses. The garden was looking fantastic, but it would take some careful planning for Nun's family because the rotational planting was only now being started. They would have to eat carefully for some time to come.

One day, a deeply respected old man came to Kainkali and Piari. "We are going to the top of the mountain to worship God and to sacrifice. Please join us. Your father would have," he urged. Both young men turned down the invitation without looking the old man in the eye. The old man then turned to the man beside him and sighed, "Nun would be sad."

That night the sky was clear, and the stars shone their exuberance, glowing with a pure white light. Well before dawn, Sanison was cooking the family food, and Piari made his way from the *manhaus* as first light began to take the power from the starlight.

Piari's skin got goose bumps as he first saw and then heard them. He had always been with others when he saw the *taia kali,* and that normally included his father. His mind turned quickly to his father, whom he still missed terribly. He thought of the times around the fire at night when his father would hold their hair and say, "*Idi hup* [God holds your hair]. If you do something wrong, the God who lives in the land of mystery will place a heavy burden on your heads."

He recalled how his father taught Kainkali and him by telling story after story. These stories would teach them not to steal, not to commit adultery, not to tell lies, not to pass on rumors that can cause fights. "If you do those things," Nun would say, "you will have a short life. People will come and kill you." Then Piari thought about the invitation to worship God given him just yesterday. He looked up at these beautiful beings. They returned his gaze, but with sadness. Then they flew away.

"Isn't it wonderful that the garden was finished in time?" Sanison said without turning as she heard her brother come to the doorway. She could easily recognize her brother's footsteps, even if he was a famed warrior who could walk without making a sound. And as her brother bent low through the doorway, she continued, "Now there is deep moisture in the *kaukau* mounds before the dry season commences. Our food will grow well." No response. That was not like her brother, who was as quick with his mind and tongue as he was with his weapons.

She looked up. "What's wrong?"

Should I tell her what I just saw? Piari thought to himself.

"Oh, nothing," he replied.

Chapter Nineteen

Don't cut down those trees," Piari yelled at some young boys who were wanting to try out a modern axe. "The spirits live among those trees," he finished forcefully. The boys ran away. No one tangled with Piari!

Omens and superstition continued to grip Piari and most of his family and clansmen. The stories handed down from their ancestors of a great and powerful God with eyes and ears and who cared about them were pushed aside. By his mid to late teens, Piari was not only a famed and fearsome warrior, but he was also known down the valley for building spirit-worship houses. Tribal warfare continued to plague the people of the Lagaip Valley. Piari's strength and skill increased year by year.

The government sent Papua New Guinean policemen into the Lagaip Valley to bring law and order. "Why do they bother us?" Piari asked angrily as the men of the village sat in a circle one night. "We do not need the government. The Piolai and Kaipi clans of the Piapri tribe can care for themselves."

He did not see that the old men had something else on their minds. An old man spoke up. "Piari, the birds and possums all make a family. Without the family, their kind would come to an end." There was a long pause as the story sunk in. Piari got the hint but was not willing to admit it. He was speechless, a rare thing indeed.

"We are your uncles, and your father would want us to help you find a bride. As we do not always marry within the tribe, have you seen any girl from neighboring tribes, or even from the tribe of your mother, whom you would like to take as a bride?"

Piari was out of his depth with this discussion. But his wit enabled him to work around it. His uncle's story gave him an idea. "Thank you, Uncle. A man possum will go in search of a lady. So I will search and tell you when I find one. Then my uncles can talk with her and her family to determine whether she is to be the one." He had no time for girls. He was Piari the fighter, Piari the warrior! And so he successfully skirted the matter of taking a wife—for now.

One cloudy day, as the wind roared through the trees, swaying branches dangerously from side to side, the head of the police came to the village. He advised the people that the government had allowed some new people to come into their valley. These people taught about God. *What was this all about? Is this a bad omen?* thought Piari.

But when the Roman Catholic missionaries came, it sounded much like what the ancestors had handed down from generation to generation. The people already believed in a personal God who lived in the land of mystery. They believed that God had a law. They even had a story about a young woman who gave birth to a child before she had ever slept with a man.

Piari decided he would have a liaison with these Christian missionaries, because they were gaining support from all the clans and tribes in the valley. He was not going to get personally involved, though. For any warrior, strategy was as important as prowess. Meanwhile, the Roman Catholic missionaries were glad to have positive support from this famed and strong young warrior.

The ties between Nun's children and their mother's clan at Yakananda had become very strong because of the time they had spent there. Thus, travel between the families was common. One day, Lamu arrived at Niungu.

What joy came to Sanison, Kainkali, Piapin, and Piari to see their cousin! Piari found Nala and said, "Come! Meet your cousin from Yakananda. He is the one I told you about who went with me to Wabag. We worked together building the *ples balus*."

The stories went late into the night. Lamu reported that the government had brought their people back to Wabag because they said the great war had finished. And the *ples balus* at Wabag had been finished last dry season. Many planes were flying into Wabag from the east.

Included in those stories as the night wore on was the news that there were different Christian groups coming into the Enga region. In addition to the Roman Catholics, there was a group of missionaries called Lutherans. It seemed that their beliefs were similar. But although both groups prayed, the Lutherans did not pray to the mother of the special child. And there was another group that had set up a school at a place called Rakamanda, southwest of Wabag. These missionaries did not believe in fighting and did not eat pigs. But they did teach the stories of the Bible and the law of God. The children in their school learned the language of the white men and received clothes from them.

"Are you serious? No fighting and no pig meat? Well, forget them!" Piari decided emphatically. But Piapin felt compelled to talk further with Lamu about the school at Rakamanda. He liked the idea of the clothes that he remembered Jim

The Fighter

Taylor wearing. Everyone was surprised when Piapin announced one night, "I am going back with Lamu. I am going to school."

"You are doing no such thing, Piapin!" Kainkali said sternly.

"Absolutely not!" agreed Piari. "You are too young to leave our village. And you do not know anything about the tribe at Rakamanda or the people that run that school. It is a long way for us to come and rescue you."

"My mind is made up," said Piapin resolutely. Obviously, strength of mind was a characteristic of this whole family. "The more I hear Lamu talk about the Christians at Rakamanda, the more I think they are closer to the stories of our father."

"But they won't fight or eat pig," Piari argued.

"Nor did father fight. And he said the food from the garden was best. He only had pig on the rarest of occasions, when there was a big feast," said Piapin.

Sanison knew her brothers and that it was useless to argue when one of them had made up his mind. She did not want to let go of her younger brother, but the elders had put him through the initiation, and he, too, was now considered a man.

As Lamu and Piapin headed out of the village, Kainkali and Piari walked with them for some time. These two older brothers, as would a father, urged much counsel on Piapin.

"Care for our brother," Piari said to Lamu.

Lamu responded earnestly, "As my own brother. I will walk with him to Wabag and beyond. I will be sure he is safe at the school."

As the two travelers moved out on their own, Piapin excitedly yelled back, "I will come back and tell you all about it!"

Piari said out loud but to no one in particular, "But those Christians don't believe in fighting. And they don't eat pig!"

Fact File

The eye-catching Papua New Guinea national flag depicts the Southern Cross-a common sight in the night sky of the Southern Hemisphere-on a black triangle, and a yellow bird of paradise, the national emblem on a red triangle.

Chapter Twenty

But Father, I want to marry this boy!" screamed Puwan. Her father was not to be moved. He turned to the rest of the *bigmen* of the Piolai clan. Among them was Piari, fight leader.

"There has never been a marriage between the Aowl and Piapri tribes, and there never will be," Piari said firmly. He continued with an Engan *tokbokis*. "A dog comes up and for no reason bites you. Is that dog your friend or enemy? Do you trust that dog? By no means. No matter how many times it might wag its tail, you can never trust it." Piari looked at Puwan. "Whomever you marry, Puwan, becomes our family. We must trust them, and they must trust us. We must be prepared to give our lives for the members of the tribe into which you marry. The Piapri could *never* trust the Aowl!"

Those heated and dogmatic words were enthusiastically endorsed by all present. That was the end of the matter.

One morning some time later the day dawned with a beautiful golden reflection on the trees and shrubs. The dazzling sunshine dissipated the cold morning mist. But this particular day, no matter how warm the sun might shine, the hearts of the Niungu village of the Piolai clan were cold and angry. Fiercely angry! Hysterically angry!

Tribal warfare could be triggered by something as simple as stealing food or land or killing a pig. But this—this was the worst crime of all! Puwan hid in her mother's hut, shamed beyond anything that could ever happen to a person. She had been raped by the man who had wanted to marry her.

One man with strong lungs was chosen to climb to the top of the ridge and declare the fight to everyone in the valley. "We are coming—coming to fight the Aowl to the death. Look out, Aowl. A dog that bites another dog is not fit to be called a dog. It should die! We and all our allies are coming to fight. No one in all your tribe will be safe." This echoed down the valley. Each tribe sent its chosen man to the top of a ridge, and so the message of the fight was passed on and on.

The Aowl were not to be outdone. They, too, declared from valley to valley their readiness for the fight. It was one of the largest and fiercest fights in living memory. Multiple clans of the Piapri tribe joined in, some who did not normally fight the Aowl. Men fell—most wounded, but some killed.

Before the sun came up each day, the Piolai clan warriors were building up their anticipation. Glistening with pig grease, they stood around small fires in the open telling stories of battle and chanting to prepare their minds and bodies for the fight ahead.

"You are a true fight leader, Piari," one warrior said. "You have killed two Aowl. And you have wounded more of the enemy than all of us put together." Piari had indeed exacted a heavy toll on the enemy.

But there were casualties at home as well. A *bigman* was killed. Taop was seriously wounded. And some older warriors were shot by arrows. The fighting took a toll on the entire village. The women tended the pigs and cared for the gardens as much as they could, ever under the watchful eye of guards.

Meanwhile, Piapin's school year had come to an end, and he came home to visit. Everyone was excited to see him and hear his many stories!

Piapin was a strong young man, and Piari asked him to join them in the fight. He assured Piapin that he would watch out for him and protect him. But Piapin refused. He said that fighting was not God's way and that killing was wrong.

Piari was angry and burst out, "If we do not stand up for our women and our whole tribe, all will be lost! The only way our tribe has any future is if we aggressively protect both our people, our land, and our name!"

Deep inside, Piari wasn't sure whether his anger at Piapin was real or was his own way of dealing with an inner voice that told him Piapin was saying exactly what his father used to say. "That school you are attending is making you weak, Piapin." And with that, Piari went off to make further plans for battle.

There seemed to be no end to this fight. The new government station in Laiagam was very close to Piari's village. The police came and warned the Niungu village and other Piolai clansmen that they must stop fighting and allow the government to catch the rapist and punish him the government way.

"No!" declared Piari. "This is our daughter. This is our honor. This is our way."

The Piapri made forays into Aowl land, burning houses, destroying gardens, and ringbarking trees. As Piari and his people knew well, destroying gardens and ringbarking trees would impact the enemy far into the future.

The government seemed powerless to stop this horrific fight. No *kiap* had yet been appointed to Laiagam, but the police had been sent to begin the work of government. And this fighting was one thing that needed to be addressed if there was to be an economic and political future for this region.

The police turned up again at Niungu village, this time with an ultimatum:

The Fighter

"Stop fighting, or you will be put in prison!" the head police officer barked.

The fighting continued unabated.

Then one day, a large police force showed up early in the morning. As fight leader, Piari was taken into custody. Nobody knew what to do. Should they fight the police? All knew how much damage the policemen's guns could do. On a previous visit to the region, a policeman shot some troublemakers, and the sight of those shot and killed caused even the warriors to tremble!

Piari was locked in the prison compound. The police had been given clear instructions to break this young warrior. "Here is a copra bag, Piari. Go on, take it!" ordered the head policeman. Piari reached out and took this large bag.

"Bring it here!" yelled another officer who was standing near a pile of sand. "Fill the bag with this sand." Piari obeyed these unusual instructions. It seemed simple and harmless enough. Once the bag was full, the officer ordered another policeman to bring two buckets of water. The officer took each bucket and poured the water into the bag of sand.

"Tie the top of the bag." Piari complied.

"Now, lift this bag of wet sand onto your shoulder and carry it to the far end of the compound," the officer ordered.

Piari was an extremely strong and fit young man. At twenty-two, he could carry as heavy an object as any man—even this extremely heavy wet sand. His pride was such that he would not show any emotion, and he would prove that he could do it.

He started out toward the far end of the prison compound. Then the officers started hitting him with their heavy wooden clubs. They beat him all the way to the end. Then he had to return with the bag, being beaten all the way. This happened every day for a week.

Each day, Piari would shout in defiance, "I am Piari. I will fight!"

But each night in the quiet of his prison cell, Piari felt the pain of his strained muscles and nursed his wounds. And he thought about his life.

My father and mother taught me about God and His ways. They taught me all I needed to know about life. I did not listen to them, and look what is happening to me! I have turned my back on my parents' advice. I have rebelled against the government's laws. I have rebelled against God's laws. I have been wrong.

At the end of the week, Piari was released from prison.

What would happen to Piari the fighter now?

Chapter Twenty-One

Pigs everywhere. Hundreds of them.

People everywhere. Thousands of them.

Men, with human hair wigs decorated in many ways, swayed to the beat of their *kundu* drums. Women chanting and dancing.

"Remember your commitment, Piari." It was his sister and younger brother. Privately, Sanison and Piapin had discussed the surprising change that had come over Piari. They were nervous that even the slightest provocation at the compensation ceremony would cause the deep distrust and anger to spill over into violence. They were concerned that this decision Piari had made was only outward. Was he changed inside?

Over many days, hundreds and hundreds of pigs changed hands as the peace and compensation process took place. But the days were filled with heavy rain, increasing the tension. Rivers of mud oozed through everything and everyone in the neutral ground offered by an adjoining neutral tribe. The police showed a very strong presence.

Miraculously, peace was achieved—for the moment. Usually, once compensation was addressed by both parties, the matter was forgotten and everyone moved on. But the Piapri and Aowl tribes remained bitter enemies.

Piari had watched the first Christian missionaries into his area for a couple of years now because they had their mission station nearby. He would often go into their sacred meeting place, past the young highland man standing at the door, and toward the altar at the front, where the mass took place. Candlelight caused shadows to play on the walls and roof. There was a peace and tranquility inside this place that felt very different from what was going on inside his heart.

He decided that for his father's sake, he would join this group. As a reward, he received from the priest salt, clothes, a knife, and a small axe. He took on the religion with relish, regularly praying to Mary: "O, Mary, mother of Jesus, you who are in heaven and close to the sun. Mary, please watch over us. Please rid us of our sicknesses. Please look after the children . . ."

In this religion, the priest was an essential link between God and the people.

The Fighter

Only they could offer the mass to the people. *The priest is like a* bigman, thought Piari. *I am considered a* bigman *of my tribe. My father was respected as a* bigman, *especially as a spiritual leader. Maybe it is time I became a* bigman *in this church.*

Never halfhearted and ever the leader, Piari approached Father Bush, the priest at the church-run school not far away at Wanpap. "I have decided to be a priest," he said.

Father Bush was surprised. "Well, that is a good desire, my son. But I am afraid that is not possible. It is not possible for a Papua New Guinean to become a priest," he said. The look on Piari's face brought fear into the priest's heart. He quickly added, "But once you are married, you can be a catechist [teacher]." That was the end of the matter.

The government began to build an airstrip at Laiagam. While that was happening, they finished building a small road between Wabag and Laiagam. The outside world was fast coming to the Lagaip Valley. And part of that outside world were more Christian missionaries. A different Christian church began work in Laiagam. Sanison began attending and joined that church.

Sometime later, right out of the blue, Piari announced to his sister, "I will come to church with you today." That morning, he heard the pastor of his sister's church say, "Men are not of heaven, but just of this earth."

Piari, as sharp of mind as ever, thought, *Well, if that is true, then I can no longer be part of the church that I have been attending. Their message is that the priest is different from all the people. No one has an automatic right to be chief in our tribe. The right to be a* bigman *is earned through fighting prowess or through business dealings or through oratory. The* bigman *is really just one of the people. Maybe the priest should be the same.*

He continued attending his sister's church, where he met a number of Engans from different tribes. One young lady, more than ten years younger than himself, had the name Kinduruwan (frost/ice girl). She was from the Wailangi tribe, a neighboring tribe to the Piapri. This girl had been born during the severe frost. It meant something to Piari, but only because this was the very time when Nun, his dear father, had died.

Deep down, Piari was not settled. His heart had not been moved. Something just was not right. As he talked with his cousin Nala one day, it came to him.

"Many stories of all these Christian missionaries sound similar to those of our ancestors. And they talk about God's law. But they still do things that shouldn't be done," said Piari.

"Like what?" Nala asked.

"Well, they all smoke and eat pig—even the priests and pastors. And they don't have any problem with us fighting. But you know that my father was a strong man who believed in God. He said that our lives must follow God in every way."

Nala reflected, "Well, your brother Piapin, what does he call himself now? Peter Piapin? He says that the Christians who run his school are different from the other Christians. These do not smoke, drink alcohol, or allow tribal fighting."

"Yes," said Piari. "But that is a hard road. I am not sure I want to walk on that road. It seems that all those Christians do is walk around with God's book and talk about what that book has to say."

Nala said, "But is that a bad thing? Your father was strong about God and His ways. Maybe following God's book and the law that is found in it is the right way. They are the same as the teachings that our fathers have handed to us from their fathers."

Piari was silent. And that was not something Nala had experienced very often. He decided he had better drop all this. "Anyway, I'll see you later, Piari. I need to go and cut some firewood." Nala was married now and had a family to care for.

Piari, the warrior, was still silent—unusually silent. He was thinking.

Fact File

Christianity comes to Papua New Guinea

The government's approach to the introduction of Christian missions in Papua New Guinea was very cautious. Each missionary group was allocated specific areas. Some time went by before more than one Christian church was allowed in an area.

This resulted in much conflict because the predominant Christian group often believed no others had a right to be there. Such attitudes and tension still exist in some areas to this day.

On July 1, 1946, the government began to allow Christian missions to enter specified areas in the Wabag region.

History of Seventh-day Adventist Church missions in Papua New Guinea, Part 1:

The first Seventh-day Adventist missionaries to Papua New Guinea, Pastor and Mrs. S. W. Carr and Fijian school teacher Peni Tovadi, arrived in 1908. They commenced their work at Bisiatabu in the Kokoda region, north of Port Moresby. It took six years before they saw the first converts baptized.

But this was in a very different and distant part of Papua New Guinea from where Piari lived. It was not till nearly forty years later that the Seventh-day Adventist Church entered the Engan region of the country.

Chapter Twenty-Two

Piari the fighter had made a commitment not to fight anymore. But another fight was going on, one that had been raging ever since he was a little boy. Superstition and fear of Timango, the devil, had been shooting arrows into his heart and mind. He had been fighting against his father's belief in God. He had been fighting against his father's belief in God's law.

The heavy smoke from the fire this particular night increased its warmth. The black encrusted framing timber and underside of the roof made the darkness inside the hut even darker. Piari was thinking deeply and felt dark inside.

Then, noticing the slowly lapping yellow flames and deep red embers in the fireplace, his heart began to lift. Light and joy began to break asunder his darkness. Deep within, hope began to emerge!

One day, the pastor drew a picture on the blackboard. It showed two roads. One road was wide and easy, with many people on it. He drew a pig and a kina shell near this road, as he knew the Engans liked them. The other road was narrow, and he drew a picture of Jesus standing close to a cross.

The pastor explained, "Jesus chose a hard road. While there are many people on the easy road, with pigs and kina, Jesus asks us to walk with Him on the hard road."

Light flashed into Piari's mind as if someone had thrown heaps of dry grass onto the night fire, making it burst into brightness. He walked out of that meeting convinced: *The Seven De Sios is on the right road, the Jesus road, the hard road. We Engans like our pig and our kinas. But Jesus died on the hard road. Both the first church I attended and my sister's church, though good people, cannot be for me as they walk on the easy road.* The fight within Piari was still there, but it was turning in God's favor.

One morning, Sanison came searching for Piari out in the bush, where he had gone hunting. He heard her calling and was concerned that something serious had happened. But then he saw what the excitement was all about.

"Piapin, my brother, you have returned. And how you have grown!" Piari loved his family deeply and missed his younger brother. Piapin, with a great big grin, raced over to his brother and held him tight. He had returned home for the year-end school break.

"I have many questions for you, little brother. But these must wait," said Piari. "Join me on the hunt."

That night Piari asked question after question of his brother, who had been learning very much at school. After answering many questions, and noting that many of Piari's questions were about God and God's ways, Piapin said, "The answers are in the book called the Bible." He pulled a small Bible out of his *billum* and held it reverently. "The stories in this book match those of our father and those of our ancestors. But in here they become even clearer, and they tell us about the Promised One—Jesus."

Piapin read from the first chapter of Genesis, describing the creation of the world. He then read from the New Testament's description of Jesus as the Creator. He showed from the Bible how God made the Sabbath day sacred.

These young men talked and read into the night. "I am like a *muruk* who has found the tree with the blue berry," Piari excitedly told his brother. "I want to eat and eat and eat." The battle was waging. Piari the fighter was in the middle of the battle, but he was not the one fighting. God and Timango were fighting over him!

The next morning, Piari declared that he would set aside some of his family land for the Seventh-day Adventist Church. God was beginning to win the battle over Piari. But He still had some way to go to win the battle for his heart.

"Piapin, I am coming with you this time when you return to school," said Piari.

The following Sunday, Piari went to his sister's church as usual. He asked the pastor about the fourth commandment, which says to keep the seventh-day Sabbath holy. "Oh, that belongs to the *Seven De* Church," was the response. This confirmed Piari's plans to bring a Seventh-day Adventist missionary to his village.

With a rough dirt road now constructed by the new government, the walk to Rakamanda did not take as long as it used to. But Piari and Piapin used every step of the way to continue their dialogue about God and God's teachings.

Upon arrival at Rakamanda, the strong young warrior, Piari, declared, "I have come to get a missionary."

"And who are you?" asked John Newman, the Australian pastor in charge of the work in that region.

"It is me, Piari," was the reply. "I am giving ground to the *Seven De Sios* Church in my village near the government center of Laiagam. I need a missionary to teach my people."

Piari was a man of action. And so were the leaders of the church. Pastor Newman approached a young single boy from Henganofi, a place ten times farther east of Wabag as Laiagam was to the west.

"Irau, will you go with Piari to Laiagam and set up God's work in his village?" Without hesitation, Irau agreed to go.

Once back at Niungu, Piari set about to build a house for Irau and a sacred place, a church, for worship. "You can live in my house until yours is ready," he told Irau. Day and night he and Irau were cutting timber, constructing, weaving pandanus leaves, cutting *kunai,* clearing ground for a garden . . .

But this was not happening in some isolated hiding place. It was good ground, and everyone knew what was going on.

His village was upset. "Send this man back to his home, Piari. We do not want another Christian mission here. We do not want the *Seven De* here!" Anger was mounting.

Normally everyone would pitch in and help. That is the Engan way. But no one helped at all. Not even his sister's church.

After much effort, the sleeping house and the place of worship were complete.

"It has been three months now," Irau said to Piari. "I must go to Rakamanda to report on the work that has been done thus far."

Piari smiled and said, "You go." This young missionary from Eastern Highlands was a good man and a hard worker. "But please return quickly. We still have much to do."

That night, Piari lay in front of the fire and thought about all that both Piapin and Irau had taught him.

God is like a warrior, he thought. *He has a plan in His battle against sin and Timango. And He will not stop. I like God a lot.*

Was Piari the fighter starting to let God do the fighting?

Fact File

History of Seventh-day Adventist Church missions in Papua New Guinea, Part 2:

Pastor Laurence Gilmore, serving as an Australian paramedic officer during World War II, walked into Wabag in the Enga region in June 1944 to assess a reported outbreak of dysentery. He is the first known Seventh-day Adventist to set foot in the Enga.

June 4, 1947: Pastors F. T. Maberly and L. I. Howell made an exploratory visit to the Enga by air, leaving two national missionaries behind to begin work.

By November 1947, teachers had commenced a school at Rakamanda, and Pastor Maberly had arrived with his family to lead the work.

History of Seventh-day Adventist Church missions in Papua New Guinea, Part 3:

The enthusiasm of the pioneers of the Seventh-day Adventist Church work in Papua New Guinea went well ahead of government protocols.

At the invitation of the people of Sopas, west of Wabag, a school and church were established in 1949. But on December 30 of that year, the Wabag District Government Office sent a letter to Pastor Frank Maberly ordering the missionaries to be withdrawn.

The church leaders lobbied higher levels of government, and finally, on March 31, 1950, were given permission to continue.

Chapter Twenty-Three

What is that commotion? Piari instinctively reached for his bow and arrows. Within seconds, he was outside the low door of his hut. The glow was intense as the new church and house burned before his eyes. The smoke gave the scene a smell, and the crackling of the fire gave sound. But Piari's anger burned hotter than any burning building.

The warrior within him came to the fore. He was angry. He searched for some indication of who did this terrible thing. Onlookers knew Piari. Someone would die for this. Piari the fighter. Piari the warrior! He would find the culprits and make them pay. Fear froze the hearts of the local people. Piari was still a highly respected and feared warrior.

The next day, as the heat subsided leaving just ashes, Piari searched for anything of Irau's few personal effects that might be saved. Nothing. Everything was burnt to a cinder by the intensity of the fire. But wait—what was that under those ashes over there? Piari pushed aside the black and powdery gray ash. *Is this possible?* he thought. *It is a miracle!*

There, unburned, was Irau's Bible. Everything had been turned to ash except the Bible.

Piari heard the sound of a small motorcycle arriving. He turned. "Hello, Mr. Dennis," he greeted. Mr. Dennis, the *kiap,* had heard of the fire and knew this was going to mean real trouble. Piari, renowned for his payback and killing, would be seeking revenge.

"Who did this?" Mr. Dennis asked.

"I don't know," Piari answered.

"What was lost?"

"Everything, Mr. Dennis. Both of the new buildings and everything in them—except for this!" And Piari held up the Bible that the fire had not even touched.

"Where was it?"

"Here." Piari led him to the spot where the Bible had been laying in the middle of the ash where some of the fiercest heat had burned everything. This miracle

The Fighter

was a clear message to Piari that the Seventh-day Adventist Church was a Christian church that was true to the Bible.

"You let *me* find the culprit, Piari. I don't want trouble," said Mr. Dennis emphatically. He could see Piari holding his bow and arrows. Piari looked at the *kiap* as he fought a battle within. After some moments of hesitation, and to the surprise of the government official, he finally said, "You take care of it, Mr. Dennis." And Piari set about cleaning up and rebuilding the house and the church.

This event was big news around the region. People expected Piari to find the arsonist and kill him. And so it was quite a sight to see the warrior putting all his energy into rebuilding rather than payback. Among those watching were girls from his sister's church, where Piari had attended.

But some of the local people mocked him. They yelled, "Who is cooking for you, Piari?" This was a local way of being rude and saying that no one cared about him.

Piari yelled in return, "I work now and eat later."

One of the girls reported to her uncle what was happening. He replied, "Well, *you* help him, Kinduruwan."

So she did. Kinduruwan helped with the building and cooked for Piari and Irau. These men worked every waking hour to reconstruct the Seventh-day Adventist church and the missionary's house.

Finally, the buildings were again completed.

But then, one night the arsonist struck again. There were people who were determined to stop the work of the Seventh-day Adventist Church in the Lagaip Valley!

This time the local people and Mr. Dennis were sure that the warrior instinct would burst out of Piari and exact vengeance. Fear haunted all who knew Piari the warrior.

But God was winning the battle for Piari's heart. "Let's get working," Piari said to Irau. So for the third time, they built the church and the house. Kinduruwan helped again as well.

Kinduruwan's uncle talked to her about the *Seven De Sios*. Although he was not a Seventh-day Adventist, he told her that she should join that church, as it was the church of the Bible—God's true church. The unburned Bible had made a great impression on him, and it created a lot of talk in the valley for a long time. Some remember it to this day!

"You must go to school, Kinduruwan," said her uncle one day. So she set out on the long walk to Rakamanda, where she could attend a Seventh-day Adventist school.

Once things settled at Niungu, Piari went on a journey himself. He noted that Kinduruwan was there learning at Rakamanda. But he continued even farther east to Moruma in the Chimbu region, taking many days to get there. This was where his younger brother Peter Piapin had gone. There he found some younger cousins who encouraged him to join them even farther east at a Seventh-day Adventist school at Kabiufa, in the Eastern Highlands region. Piari was a grown man now, but he wanted to learn. So he slept in the school's *hauskuk* for three months so he could attend classes.

While sleeping there, one night he had a dream. He saw a boy holding a book. This boy was told to go and tell the story of that book. So the boy yelled out, "*Taim bilong Jisas I kam!*" (Jesus is coming soon!)

Some boys shook him to wake him up. "You are yelling out," they said.

What does this mean? Who is the boy in my dream? Surely it's not me! While his head accepted God's truth, his heart was not yet ready. God had still not yet won the battle for Piari's heart.

Piari retraced his steps westward and went on the long journey back to Rakamanda, where Kinduruwan was in school. He began classes there.

One day a boy came to Piari. "The headmaster, Mr. Oemcke, wants to see you." Piari, this muscular young man with a broad smile, bounced up to the headmaster.

"Do you want to go to school, or do you want to work?" asked Mr. Oemcke.

"I am easy either way," said Piari, not sure what this direct question really meant. *I wish Mr. Oemcke would tell me a* tokbokis. *Then I might understand better.*

"Then take this letter to Pastor Campbell, the senior missionary at Tetemanda. It introduces you as the teacher of the little children." Piari still didn't fully understand, but the smile on Mr. Oemcke's face encouraged him to take the letter. God was leading this young warrior ever closer to His heart and His plan for his life.

And so Piari, the famed and feared warrior, began to teach little children how to read and write. But as time went by, Pastor Campbell noticed something happening at every lunch time. Piari was getting out the picture roll, a flip chart with beautiful pictures of stories from the Bible. This young warrior, himself not yet baptized, was enthusiastically telling these stories to the children and encouraging them to follow Jesus. He even preached to the children, his hands telling the story just as excitedly as his voice.

At long last, God had clearly won the battle for Piari Nun. This proud and strong tribal fighting man had died to self and had learned to love and serve God—the same God his father had tried to teach him to follow when he was a boy. "I am ready to be baptized now," Piari declared. He returned to Niungu and declared his lifelong faith in Jesus through baptism, being in the first group to be baptized and becoming Seventh-day Adventists in his home area.

He kept his name, Piari. But he also took on another name, the name of a Bible warrior—Paul. As the story of the feared warrior Piari ended, the story of Paul Piari, God's warrior, was just beginning. And it was a story even more exciting! That is what happens when you choose to let God win the battle for your heart.

Fact File

History of Seventh-day Adventist Church missions in Papua New Guinea, Part 4:

Seventh-day Adventist missionary pioneers, many of whom came from other Pacific nations, sought every opportunity to expand God's work. Church growth gained momentum over time.

Today, the work of the Seventh-day Adventist Church is found throughout the whole of Papua New Guinea.

The 2010 official government records show that 10 percent of the population declare themselves Seventh-day Adventists, the fourth largest church in the nation.

(Twenty-seven percent are Roman Catholic, 19.5 percent are Evangelical Lutheran, and 11.5 percent are United Church.)

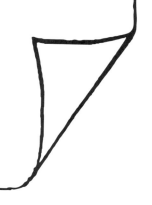

Epilogue

Kinduruwan's uncle talked with Piari and then with Kinduruwan. It was agreed and the announcement was made: Piari and Kinduruwan would be married. Over the course of their married life, these two would see immense change take place in their region and throughout all of Papua New Guinea.

Paul Piari was ordained as a pastor of the Seventh-day Adventist Church in 1967. He and Kinduruwan, who took on the Christian name Dorcas, served as pioneer missionaries to many locations around Papua New Guinea. Paul Piari was eventually able to travel the world, telling the story of what God has done for him and his people.

He was always a man to take the lead. He never turned and ran but faced whatever enemy came his way. He was a fighter through and through. But when he let God win the battle for his heart, he began fighting for God and did it God's way, ever wanting others to know this God who loved him so much that He died for him.

Piari was never once seriously wounded in all his tribal fighting. But as a warrior for God, he was attacked and physically injured by enemies of God's truth on numerous occasions. Piari, the fighter, never fought back. He counted injury for his God as an honor.

He retired after nearly thirty years of service.

In 2010, Pastor Paul, God's warrior, died of injuries after being accidently hit by a car while he was crossing the road in Port Moresby, the capital of Papua New Guinea. As God had indicated to him while still a boy before the Christian missionaries ever came to his valley, he died as an old man with white hair.

Paul Piari died with a strong belief that Jesus is coming again soon. He will be there on that resurrection day.

Will you be there? Turn your life over to Jesus. Follow Jesus wherever He leads you. And as well as seeing Jesus on that resurrection day, you can also say hello to Paul Piari, who changed from being a tribal warrior who killed people to God's warrior who loved leading people to Jesus and their salvation.

You may have to stand in line to greet Pastor Paul Piari. I am sure others will want to greet him, such as his father, Nun, and his mother, Titam. How joyfully surprised they will be to find that after they died, their son stopped killing and instead became God's warrior! What a day that will be!

Glossary

alamand or *alamandiooo:* Engan language for "Good afternoon." The Engan way of speaking often holds the "o" on the end of words, especially greetings. This is to give real expression to such greetings.

animists: A worldview that God or a spiritual essence is actually in the animate and inanimate, such as trees, stones, animals, and birds. In some places, it carries along with it a belief in ancestral spirits aligned with these elements. Some believe that if these spirits are placated, they might help rather than harm people.

billum: A string bag woven by hand from bush string. Women gather bush fibers from vine and bark and roll them together into long pieces of string. It is a very labor-intensive task, but the end result is a very long-lasting bag. Both men and women use *billums,* but with different designs for different uses. Women carry babies in *billums,* as well as loads of garden produce weighing up to sixty-five pounds.

gote mau piya pelyo: Literally translated, "going to make the God *mumu.*" It was used in connection with a regular ceremony that was like a sacrifice to God, where God would in turn communicate with the family leaders through this ceremony and indicate what the future had in store for them.

kaukau: Also known as sweet potato, a tuber that grows under a ground-hugging vine. This is a staple food for all highland areas of Papua New Guinea.

kina and *toea:* Shells of saltwater shellfish traded from tribe to tribe, starting with the coastal tribes. As tribes trade these with their more inland neighbors, the value grows. All tribes, but particularly the tribes of the isolated highland valleys, place great value on these shells, especially the kina shell. Today, *kina* and *toea* are the names given to the Papua New Guinean currency. There are one hundred *toea* in one *kina*.

kunai **grass:** A long-bladed grass, sometimes rising to six feet in height. This grass was cut at a little over three feet and laid in bunches on rough roof trusses, with the grassy heads facing downward. It proves to be an effective protection from rain as well as reasonable insulation. *Kunai* grass is also very combustible and generates extreme heat.

kundu: A slender, elongated drum unique to the Enga region. It is hollowed out of a single piece of timber, then fitted with snakeskin tightly over the top. The skin is tied on by vines and allowed to dry. As it dries, it shrinks, providing tautness. As the fingers pound the skin, the sound vibrates down the long, thin drum, resulting in strong midtone resonance.

mumu: a Melanesian Pisin term for an underground oven. The actual method of preparing a *mumu*, along with food preparation and cooking methods, varies throughout the various cultures of Papua New Guinea. The Engan style of *mumu* involves digging a large hole in the ground and placing at its base extremely hot stones that have been heated on a large fire. The food is usually wrapped in banana leaves and placed on top of these stones. Hot stones are again placed on top, and then earth is packed in on top. Everyone anticipates the opening, as the aroma of cooked food bursts out as the process is reversed.

muruk: Cassowary, a handsome flightless bird with a body standing more than three feet tall and a long neck that can reach up another thirty inches. It has a large bone helmet on top of its head, enabling it to crash through jungle undergrowth without doing itself any damage. Its central toe has an elongated spike on it of up to five inches. This is used to forage, but in defense it is a dangerous weapon that can disembowel another animal or a person.

Nala: The name of Piari's best friend. *Nala* in the Engan language means "the one who eats."

pitpit: The name for the family of grasses that grows throughout Papua New Guinea. The stem of a species that grows well over six feet tall in the Enga Province is used for weaving walls and mats. It is split and opened up for hand weaving. Another much shorter species is used for food.

Seven De Sios: Melanesian pidgin for the Seventh-day Adventist Church.

singsing: The general name for community dancing.

The Fighter

taia kali: Literally translated, "heavenly man." This is the traditional name given to angelic beings.

tanget (pronounced "tung-get"): A short branch with elongated leaves worn by men to cover their buttocks to protect their modesty. It is placed through a vine waistband to hold it in place.

taro: An underground tuber that grows from a single stem plant with large leaves. When mature, it is dug up and cooked in the ashes of the fire or boiled.

Taop: An Engan trading name parents sometimes give a child they believe will become a competent trader. It has a unique pronunciation that is challenging for those who do not speak Engan. It sounds something like "tar-op," with the central sounds coming from the back of the throat.

tribes: Social groups with their own worldview, norms, and sense of order and authority. Within Engan tribes there are clans and villages. Two clans within the Piapri tribe are the Piolai and Kaipi. The Niungu village is part of the larger Piolai clan of the Piapri tribe. While most tribal fighting occurs between tribes, sometimes there can be serious tension and even fighting between clans.

yakapalin: Engan language for "Thank you." When expressed *yakapalinoooooooo,* it is an extremely enthusiastic thank you.